DANCING

ON

COALS

DANCING ON COALS

A Memoir of an Overperformer

CYNTHIA MOORE

SHE WRITES PRESS

Published 2025
Printed in the United States of America
Print ISBN: 978-1-64742-856-3
E-ISBN: 978-1-64742-857-0
Library of Congress Control Number: 2024922583

For information, address:
She Writes Press
1569 Solano Ave #546
Berkeley, CA 94707

Interior design by Stacey Aaronson

She Writes Press is a division of SparkPoint Studio, LLC.

Names and identifying characteristics have been changed to protect the privacy of certain individuals.

Sexy ghost, a performer, a demon, a gadfly
To never have enough be enough get enough
Dancing on coals . . .

—Anne Waldman, "Sleeping with the Hungry Ghost"

For David, Kyle, and Eliza

The Language of Love

IT'S SUNDAY MORNING, AND DAVID STANDS AT THE STOVE flipping pancakes. He drops stacks of golden-brown pancakes onto the lumpy plate that our daughter Eliza made in first grade. Gusts of rain splatter against the windows, but the cheerful yellow light inside our kitchen glows buttery against the gray morning. I watch the familiar muscles of David's back ripple under his faded Costco sweatshirt; I notice the silent enthusiasm of his work, and it's as if I can see through the veils of daily life, right through the whole cover-up, and what I see is this: he is love. I stand there in my pj's, my hair a rat's nest on my head, my breath redolent with old dreams, and I'm staring at my husband's back as if it's showing me a rerun of *Miracle on 34th Street.*

David doesn't turn around. He's not the type to snuffle my neck or whisper endearments. He's a machinery man, comfortable with surface grinders that allow him precision to a thirty-second of an inch, his skin permanently dusted with fine metal shavings. He tunes the engine of my car, he buys me double-A batteries in bulk, and he rewires my ancient floor lamps. Right now, the shape of his back, bent over the frying pan on this rainy Sunday morning, speaks to me in the language of carburetors and floor lamps, the language of love. As I decipher the message his muscles spell out, a flame kindles deep in my chest. I will eat as many of those pancakes as I can. I will eat until my stomach hurts.

Later, we go for a walk in the rain with ten-year-old Eliza and her friend Celeste. We are packed to the tonsils with pancakes and dressed in way too many layers of rain gear. We scurry from the house with our heads bent over our Gore-Tex, bragging about our secret inside pockets, our sweat vents that open and close, our reversible zippers. We are bulky and proud. Celeste has borrowed my old rain boots, which are two sizes too big for her, but she doesn't complain, even when the mud sucks the boots right off her feet. This is why she's been Eliza's best friend for eight acrobatic years: Eliza would not tolerate a whiner.

My daughter grips my hand, letting go only to sidetrack through a puddle, leaving trails of giggles in her wake. David and I remember the days when she was small enough to twirl through the air between us while we held her hands and tossed her into the sky. And earlier days, when we flung her older brother over our heads. We threw our children at the clouds to teach them how to fly. *Whoop-di-doo!* we shouted as they sailed upward. I wonder if all families have secret names for things, names that invoke the squeals and smells of their special, hoarded memories.

David leads the expedition. We follow narrower and narrower trails through tangles of winterberry limbs, trails that disappear into clots of underbrush too thick to navigate. I lag behind, complaining about poison oak, sliding down muddy ninety-degree hills on my backside while David forges ahead. He adores going where no man has gone before, even if it's only the hillside behind Berkeley's Lawrence Hall of Science. We follow in the silent tracks of his joy. Scrambling under branches just two feet off the ground, we peer into fox dens and rabbit holes, lose our footing, and holler all the way down.

Even as I fret about the perils of poison oak, I am secretly delighted. "We're lost on a desert island," I announce, brushing clumps of mud from my pants. "What shall we have for dinner—sticks or leaves?"

David, just ahead, doesn't miss a beat. "How about sticks *and* leaves?" he says. And it is then, right in that crack between one minute and the next, that I know:

This is enough.

PART ONE

CHAPTER ONE

The Finishing Zoo

THE SCORCH OF SUN AGAINST THE WHITEWASHED CONCRETE burns a kind of light blindness into my vision as my bare feet dance across the powdery surface of the garage roof. I am, in my imagination, the prima ballerina of the world's greatest ballet company, and, to the hushed awe of thousands of onlookers, I leap, twirl, pirouette, and land. Plié, jeté, tour jeté, pas de chat. I flawlessly execute the steps even though I am only eleven years old.

I fly.

Pink hibiscus nod lazily on nearby bushes, and palm fronds clatter their hushed applause. The paperbark trees, the passing gulls, the climbing bougainvillea hold their breath as I soar through the air to land on the flat white roof with dirty feet. Hibiscus and mourning doves cheer: I will be great. The world awaits me with a hungry heart. I see my destiny unfurling before me like a long, red carpet, and in this secret place where the whitewashed roof forms a sun-blinded stage, I leap into my future.

The Bahamians are revolting. They are rebelling against three hundred years of British domination, and the streets boil with their rage. Pounding on goatskin drums, they chant, "Kill the whites! Kill the whites!"

I know this rage. I want to be inside it. Even though I am a child, I sense that nothing in my life will ever be this gut-felt again. The furious mob spills through our neighborhood, and strangely, it doesn't scare me; it makes me want to run out and smash things right alongside them. But I am trapped in my fine house, wondering where I belong: in the kitchen with the dark-skinned people who hold me to their bodies when I cry, or in the living room drinking Sanka with my slurry-speeched mother and hollow-eyed stepfather.

I hear them on the phone concocting delusional fantasies of escaping to Switzerland where, they have been assured, the natives are docile. They will pick their next country just as impulsively as they chose this one. In three months, we will hightail it to Geneva in a haze of misbegotten hope. It will be 1963.

First, they will ship my sister Jill off to a woodsy prep school in the States to join our three older siblings, disseminated to various boarding schools during the divorce. With stunning alacrity, they'll dispatch my developmentally disabled sister, Franny, to a cozy institution in Pennsylvania. When they eyeball me, I freeze. *Don't send me away.* An ice-cold wind blows through my gut.

"We're enrolling you in finishing school," my mother announces, and I forget how to breathe. But I pack my things, take leave of my friends, and say goodbye to the angry, sun-drenched island that has been my home. Whatever small sanctuary I have found here between the islanders' fury and my stepfather's nocturnal rages is about to evaporate.

Before I know it, the tires of our rented car crunch up the gravel drive of a dreary Swiss boarding school draped in dead vines. With my face pressed against the window, I wrestle with images of a flattened, polished self, finished within an inch of my life by Swiss spinsters wielding gigantic floor sanders. *How do you finish a person?* I wonder. *Will I shine?*

"This will be terrific," my mother burbles as she bustles me through the front door. "You'll learn French!"

I am not consoled by this pronouncement, and my stomach lurches when she shouts, "Goodbye!" and whizzes back to the rental car. She leaves me stranded in the hallway with no other option but to follow Madame Schutz, who sails ahead like a tank.

Don't cry, I instruct myself in a brook-no-nonsense voice as I shuffle down the drafty halls. Madame Schutz's lace-up shoes clatter ominously against the linoleum, and her gunmetal hair reflects the gray sky. It is a sad bump to reality for a prima ballerina. The island's exuberance has drained from my world; Switzerland is a fusty, overweight matron of a country, and I swallow the fist of my loneliness.

Madame Schutz unlocks a door and pokes me through it with a sharp finger to my shoulder blade. "This is your rhume," she says, making a room sound like a malady. "You will share it with Stephania, who speaks no English."

Stephania, like all the other girls, sports womanly curves while I, at eleven, am bony-flat. No one ever explains to me why a four-year gap separates me from the other students. (Later, I will find out that my stepfather paid a bundle of cash to shoe-horn me into high school at age eleven.)

Jiggling breasts in complicated support garments overwhelm my line of vision as I wander down the hallways, looking for warmth. Shrill chirps echo off damp plaster walls.

"*Ciao!* Lucia! *Come stai?*"

"*Bene*, Steffi! *Com'è andata la tua estate?*"

I stumble through the branchy forest of girls, dwarfed by their exuberance.

Stephania, I am dismayed to discover, bathes with all her clothes on. She digs beneath shrouds of undergarments to wash her womanly parts with a rag. She puts a screen around her bed so I can't watch her sleep. We don't talk. Our eyes, when we look at each other, are the lost eyes of animals separated from their families at birth. We are in the zoo now, the finishing zoo. We will look really good to everyone when we get out. Finally, we will be what they want us to be.

This is something to hope for.

I comfort myself with the glow of the cold moon that lights my window when I wake and the crisp, hard rolls that will still be warm from the oven. I wrap myself in the languages that begin to roll from my mouth, the swear words I learn in Hebrew, Dutch, and Armenian; the way girls from Israel, Syria, and Togo can say *penis* in ten languages. Virginal mouths wrapped around the nastiest words we can find.

Sometimes I remember the street warmth of Nassau; the hot air in my face as I rode my bike; the mangoes, the hog plums, the picnics on white beaches that bordered an emerald sea. We pedaled down the street, exhilarated, fleeing from naked rapists who lurked in the bushes, according to my best friend, Joanie Gates, who insisted that hordes of rapists were escaping like ants from the insane asylum.

I remember the haunted house where Chrissie Goosen unzipped his fly and all the girls screamed because his dangly thing looked just like a pickle. I remember the Black women who rocked me to the booming pulse of waves at night, the unspoken message passing from their bodies into mine that there was enough love to go around. "You come on over to *my* house, baby, we feed you up good." And they did feed me up, in every way they could.

I wanted to live in their houses, knit myself into their fabric, chase chickens with their grandchildren. Crouched beneath stilt houses gobbling fist-squeezed balls of Wonder Bread, I inhaled the spicy aroma of black-eyed peas simmering in charred pots. Merle and Daisy cleaned up our messes and our emotional wreckage, too. Picked us up, dusted us off, and set us back on the shelf. That was me: on the shelf, waiting for someone to find a use for me. Aside from the naked rapists, it was a fine life in which children ran barefoot and lived at home and folks didn't wash themselves behind screens with all their clothes on.

But here I am in a cold, gray classroom in Switzerland, avoiding the trajectory of Mr. Kohler's liquor-addled breath. Why is algebra important anyway? What on earth does the square root of *2x-y* have to do with going home? A wad of spinach winks at me from Mr. Kohler's gums, and my insides are as heavy as a house. Nothing can make me move my limbs. I lie in my narrow bed and cry into my stuffed dog until his ears are drenched.

Then Angela Farmer runs off with the history teacher, providing a ripple of thrill. Angela is feral, from South Carolina. We slide glances at her bitten nails and memorize the black slashes of her eyeliner as if our futures are written there. When she runs off with Mr. Hadley, we are ecstatic, slamming our doors, hissing, "What a *slut!*"

Carol Midgen teaches me the basics of making out with tongue, which she figures I will need since I am almost twelve. It's an excuse for her to tell me every detail of what she does with her boyfriend back home, pointing out the infinitesimal difference between what is acceptable (inside the bra) and what is not (inside the panties). I can't imagine any of it, never having touched a boy except during a game of kissing catchers in which I smacked Chrissie Goosen, hard and dry as toast, on the lips. It was gross, but I can't tell Carol that—she's my only friend.

We take the bus from town, where we flirt so convincingly that two boys follow us back to school. I am thrilled to feel wanted, but really, it's Carol's cantaloupe breasts that lure them onto our bus. Madame Schutz barges out on her military heels and flaps her bony fingers.

"Begone!" she cries in her raven's voice. "And no coming back!"

They scamper away, and we see with disappointment, our aching faces pressed against the glass, that they are only boys after all. Not the strong, hopeful men who will set us free. No one is strong enough to free us from this place.

I beg Mama to let me come home. I write her dozens of letters every day, blotchy with tears (and a little tap water). I write that I will wash the car and make the beds; I will sleep in the basement like a scullery maid if she will slip me a scrap of bread now and then. I will scrub, like Cinderella, and I will sleep on a pallet, whatever that is. I will make it up to her, the terrible thing I have done, as soon as I figure out what it is. I am convinced I have made a grievous mistake that has torn me from my family, and I pray to a generous, white-haired god in the sky to fix me up quick. Make me worth Mama's attention. I pretend I am a starveling with a scrub brush—what mother could say no?

Mine does.

The day she comes to visit, I crank up my despair, hoping to ignite her love. I smudge mascara under my eyes and sprawl across my bed so the first thing she sees when she walks through the door is the shape of my grief. *Oh please*, I pray as unbearable longing hollows my ribs. *Take me home with you.*

Mama swans in, taupe in Armani, glittering with hoop earrings, wearing a hat. For some reason, this makes me think of Jackie Kennedy weeping in her pink suit because they just shot her husband. Spattered with blood and bone, she never once took off her hat. Mama slams through the door and flips up the shades (which I have lowered for ambience), hauls me to my feet, and says angrily, "If you don't cut this out, I'll stop coming."

My heart ruptures inside my chest. I am free-falling, and it's bottomless. I tumble and tumble, but there is nowhere to go. Mama won't take me home with her. I am trapped between gray walls in a gray life where older girls flock like birds and I belong to no one. I am nobody. Something collapses inside me and I think, *This is it. It's finally happened: I am dead.* I sit on the bed with my smudgy eyes and the wreckage of my mother's love inside me, and I can't move my legs.

"If you refuse to be cheerful," she announces, "there's no point in my driving all this way. Stop the bloody melodrama."

I consider throwing myself into her arms. I consider strangling her with my need. But I can't move. All I can do is blink, as if my eyelids are the only part of me that work. What happened to my mama's love? Was it ever there? I'm too young to be philosophical. My eyelids are blinking up and down like malfunctioning garage doors when something hisses in my ear. It speaks with the sharp, knowing voice of someone who has always been inside me, hovering in the background like some kind of playground monitor. It cuts through my self-pity: *Shut up and pay attention.*

I sniff. I wipe my runny nose on the back of my hand. I try to figure out what it is that I'm supposed to pay attention to, and I blink, blink, blink. *Your mother is not the answer*, says the playground monitor. I peer at the woman who is my mother, currently making my bed with starchy motions, her hat bobbing perilously on her head, and that is the moment when I make up my mind.

You are not the answer, I think, and suddenly I am free. No more anguish. No more yearning. I walk through a steel door that slams shut behind me, and *poof!* I'm all grown up. I am as heartless and brisk as an efficiency expert. The relief is as sweet as huckleberry pie. As the winter sun spills watery light on the linoleum floor, I go to the sink and wash the tragedy off my face. Then, in my best Katharine Hepburn voice, I tell my mother it is time for her to leave. I don't need her anymore.

I am eleven years old and I can't afford mommy problems.

After firing my mother, I embark with ferocity on the first of many personal makeovers. I become the best algebra student, the best French speaker, the best friend of all the wiry old ladies who run the place. *"Mais, oui,* Madame Schutz!" *"Mais, non,* Mademoiselle Friselle!"

Then I scuttle behind the closed doors of my (much older) friends and shriek *zereg* (penis) in Hebrew with Yael Klein, who is Israeli, and *koos* (pussy) with Kirsten Bundt, who is Norwegian.

When I lived in Nassau, I didn't realize how precarious were the things that anchored me to happiness: a family, a room of my own, a desk where I scribbled pages of febrile poetry scrubbed pink with my eraser. I would carry my precious sonnets down the hall and hesitate before knocking at the fat white door behind which Mama and Daddy Howard did secret things. He was retired and she was horribly wealthy, so they had plenty of time to perform secret things, which she would later describe to me in prurient detail. But when they weren't closeted away in fumes of lust, my mother tied her robe, threw the door open, and allowed me in. I'd clutch my sweaty poem in one hand as I slunk into her blood-red dressing room, gaping at the gilt-framed nudes languishing on satin sheets. They had grapes and peaches where their you-knows should have been. Once, I hauled Joanie Gates in there to show her that real privates did not resemble Chrissie Goosen's pickle in any way. Real privates, I pronounced, looked like peaches.

I dragged my friends on guided tours of the garish Victorian dressing room with its ormolu clocks and swan-head fixtures. I gestured grandly at the bidet. "You wash your *butt* with it," I announced, as if I knew everything there was to know. Daddy Howard would glide past in his satin dressing gown, a tortoise-shell cigarette holder clamped in his jaw, grimacing at the beastly little females I had lugged into his boudoir. *The whole problem*, I once heard his friend Charles mention to a lunch guest, *was that Howard should have married a man.*

So there I was, cowering amid the cupids, grasping some poem I'd filled with blood. Each time, as I trembled the page toward Mama's perfectly manicured hand, I'd hope against hope that maybe she would notice me just this once. "This is wonderful," she would say, and everything would change swiftly for the better.

She was beautiful with her silky robe and her mussed hair, her stench of tobacco. She was wildly intelligent and could have been a teacher, a writer, or a nuclear physicist. When I told her this, she glared at me through slitted lids, assessing whether I was brain damaged like my sister. All she wanted was to be Howard's wife. She wanted it more than anything in the world. Our lives curled and twisted around these two irreconcilable desires. Mine: if only she could love me, and hers: if only he could love her. Our fates bore the doom of parallel lines, never to meet.

"You could make egg salad sandwiches like Joanie Gates's mom," I said, trying not to stare at my poem, crumpled in her hand, "and watch me run the three-legged race on Saturday." But nothing ever caught her interest the way Daddy Howard did with those peaches in his pants.

"Pass the scotch," she said, lining her lips ruby red. She drank to dull her desire. I dulled mine with books.

Daddy Howard, to give him credit, tried to love her. He tried so hard that his face was a mask of effort. But he couldn't. Just like he couldn't hold a job, he couldn't be an artist, and he couldn't be a daddy even though I was supposed to pretend he was my daddy. He disliked children. He tried to be something he wasn't, poor man, and only later, when I became a teenager, would I understand that pain. He and I would stay up late into the night around their Swiss kitchen table, and he would pore over his past failures as I would pore over my future failures. We would look at each other across mugs of cold coffee and see every possible permutation of disaster in each other's faces. That tenderness would briefly connect us. But then she would divorce him, and he would die alone.

There was a time when our patched-together family ballooned with hope. I was five when Mama was pregnant with Franny. Mama and Howard smoked two packs of Kents a day, and she drank throughout her pregnancy. But when Franny sat between them like a china doll, her eyes like stars, her lips like cherries, they hoped for a minute that she could save them. They drank less, fought little. It seemed like there might be enough love to go around. But there's never enough. That's the human equation. We are rats in a cage fighting over a single pellet.

And we had a secret eating us from the inside out.

Something was wrong with Franny.

When she came home from nursery school with bite marks strung like pearls along her arms, they took her to a psychiatrist. Without a smidgen of emotion, he pronounced her "severely mentally retarded." Our happiness unraveled like an old sweater. Our grief blacked out the sun. Franny and I stopped playing princesses with our socks, and Mama and Daddy Howard main-lined gin. They withdrew into separate caves of sorrow, from which they spat missiles intended to maim. Every night, the sounds of their brawling echoed down the hall to my room, where I curled into a ball and plugged my ears.

"My *other* five children are perfectly healthy."

"Your womb is dried up."

"Your sperm is damaged from booze and indiscriminate fucking."

The mushroom cloud of their fury filled the house, coating us all in poison. Howard's rage would claw at me for years. "It's *your* fault she's like this," he hissed at me. "*You* took all the brains." I took to sleeping in the linen closet, where towels kept me safe.

One morning, bleary-eyed with shame, they stared at Franny as if she were a piece of incriminating evidence. They couldn't bear to live with her, and they couldn't bear to live without her. Had I understood this at the time, I may have seen that they were staggering under the weight of their own anguish. But Franny and I were children, and neither of us comprehended that we needed to be sent away because we were living proof of their failure. We were scattered, along with our four older siblings, to the four corners of the world where dreams of family withered and died.

So here I am in Switzerland, flanked by sixteen-year-olds, realizing that I will never go home. I conclude that henceforth, I must be the best. I must be so exceptional that no one will over-look me. I nurse a dream that if I stand out, my real father will pause his twenty-four-hour executive globe-trotting long enough to be lightning-struck by my accomplishments. My real father, I should mention, runs an international corporation. He's a shooting star. I send up flares when he rockets past, but he leaves me holding a handful of stardust and wishful thinking. I wait by the phone, and sometimes he calls. As the CEO of an international enterprise, he travels at light speed around the world, leaving a litter of children in his wake. We are the price of his ambition, the products of his desires. One day—I swear—he will notice me.

That girl, he'll think, stepping into a cab in downtown Tokyo, having just read about me in the *New York Times. She's Somebody*. Not just *anybody*, God forbid. A Somebody worth knowing, worth calling on the phone, worth taking home with you at the end of the day.

I will be the kind of person that's on a list somewhere. I must get on that list. A Who's Who for the Who Are Yous.

CHAPTER TWO

You Dance like a Freshly Neutered Goat

I HAPPEN ONTO THE STAGE BY ACCIDENT. AS MY BALLET teacher's pet, I prettily pass out marshmallows to a bevy of tutu-clad six-year-olds as my entire ballet class is cast in Yul Brynner's *The King and I*. Every night I climb onto the stage at the British Colonial Hotel, my hair dyed black, skin dyed brown, to dance (oblivious to racist irony) between Yul Brynner's legs. The audience's attention is a downpour from heaven, hundreds of gallons of love dumped on my undeserving head. I stagger home like a junkie and crash into dreams of fame and fortune as I stain my sheets mahogany brown.

After that, I worm my way into every production I can find, playing toadstools and bugs, and once, at a low ebb in my career, a hole in a wall. If I have a spoken line, I rehearse it until I can say it backward standing on my head, and then I rehearse it some more, convinced that fame is the sure result of memorization. At curtain call, I sway in drunken euphoria as the applause breaks over me in waves.

When I fly to the States at fourteen to attend an all-girls boarding school in Upstate New York, I try to replace my missing family with Drama Club, which promises belonging and approval in the same heady mixture. I audition. I overact. I am rejected. I audition again, more desperately.

Imagine the scene: A hundred of us have tried out for clubs that will eke out droplets of self-worth, and we pile into a sweaty auditorium, chewing our fingers raw. Feral with anticipation, we writhe in our seats until the winners are announced, whereupon, regardless of the outcome, we erupt in hysteria. We shriek, we sob, we tear our hair. I cringe, but I don't exaggerate. As adolescent girls exiled from our families, these are the only rituals of belonging we have. Acceptance is dangled in front of us like a carnival trinket, and we will knock each other flat to grab it.

Rejected by the Drama Club, I weep into my friend's neck but awaken the next day determined to try again. I march into my audition, holler *Antigone* at top volume, and stagger out to collapse onto a bench. I am a lost fourteen-year-old bursting with fabricated passion. After my third try, the judges sigh, scratch a mark next to my name, and accept me into the Drama Club, wearied by my Antigone. When I hear the drama teacher whisper, "Cindy Moore? She works *so* hard," I figure that will be my ticket to success: I will work twice as hard as everybody else. By the time I reach forty, I will be half dead from exhaustion.

From Antioch College, at nineteen, I sign up for theater training in the Netherlands Antilles, which will culminate in a performance at La MaMa Theatre in New York. We fly down, five college boys and I, to throw sleeping bags onto the floor of a ruined manor house in Curaçao. The house, a shell of its former self, has no plumbing, no electricity, no windows or doors. We bathe in water drawn from a frog-infested well, and since we are living in the old slave section of Curaçao known as Otrabanda (the "other side"), we promptly take the name for our theater company.

A Belgian director by the name of Tone Brulin has agreed to train us in a revolutionary form of physical theater exalted by the Polish innovator Jerzy Grotowski, and we have agreed to—well, we have no idea what we've agreed to. We've jumped at the chance to escape Ohio in January, so here we are, toting ratty backpacks and squinting into blinding sun. We are going to be pioneers of avant-garde theater, sacrificing our soft beds and plug-in blow-dryers for the swampy vapors of a decrepit manor house. We sleep swathed in mosquito nets on a hard wooden floor and warm cans of chili on a hot plate. Our director, the Belgian despot, exhorts us daily to hurl our bodies at the walls *faster! harder! higher!* while shouting insults at us in a bored Belgian accent. "You stink, Stephen. You dance like a freshly neutered goat."

Morning, afternoon, and evening, we throw our broken, bleeding bodies across that wooden floor because—we've been told—true artists must be crushed. They must be walloped, fractured, and shattered in order to separate themselves from their pesky egos. All good artists (according to Gauloiseswreathed Tone) must toss their dismembered egos out the window to splat in a pulpy mess below before undertaking the hallowed, breathless rite of their art. Our hallowed, breathless rite involves throwing furniture at each other in perfect synchronization with Beethoven's Ninth Symphony. Decades later, I will still be able to sing *"Freude schöner Götterfunken, tochter aus Elysium"* like a panic-induced Pavlovian dog.

Eight a.m.: Tone, nursing takeout coffee, scowls in the window seat, pen and notebook on the scarred table before him. He hopes to capture jots of inspiration that will become our "theater piece." Roger goes first—he's the nimblest. The goal is to see how long he can last, throwing his body as hard and fast and accurately as he can from one prescribed position to the next: shoulder-stand, headstand, forward roll, flip. Backflip, cradle, elbow-stand, roll. He is bathed in sweat, bleeding from the top of his head where a blister has burst. He is going on fifty-five minutes, and it's clear he will either collapse or die before Tone calls an end to it. Finally, Roger falls into a heap and Tone grunts his approval. Next, Graham pops up and delivers a sweat-soaked fifty minutes, and then Stephen manages a dripping forty-five.

It's my turn.

I stand rigid in the center of the room, take a deep breath, focus my attention, and hurl myself into the routine: headstand, kip, shoulder-stand, dive. Elbow-stand, roll, cartwheel, candle. Thirty-five minutes later, I am drenched in sweat, gasping for air, blood pouring from my left shin. I am sucking down tears because my legs won't hold me up, and I can't let the men see my pain. I throw myself to the floor, lift into a headstand, plunge into a dive. I force myself into a shoulder-stand and tumble out in a perfect backward roll. I collapse onto the floorboards—*I did it.* Forty minutes of heart-stopping acrobatics. There is an audible exhalation, and I realize the guys have been holding their breath. We all look to Tone, awaiting his pronouncement.

"That was shit," he says.

I wipe sweat from my eyes. I must have misheard him.

"That was shit," he repeats. "Your body is like vanilla pudding. You must go faster, harder. Like a *knife.* Who's next?"

Tone's words rocket through my bones like a cancer. I force my head high as I lower myself among the boys, smelling their pity. It takes every ounce of self-control not to cry, but I *must* remain fierce, or I will dissolve. If I could reverse time, I would tell that girl to stand up and fight back. For all the women everywhere who've been told they're not good enough by men who make the rules—rules that exclude women by their very nature—I might say, *Don't talk to me that way. I deserve respect.* Or a wiser version of me might say, *I don't actually* need *your respect.* I would tell that girl there's more to life than a tyrant's approval. But that girl swallows her tears, promises to work harder, and vows to become more like a man. It's the only road to success.

"So, Nelson," I whisper that night to the diaphanous blur of mosquito netting on my left. The moon pouring through the window lights our nets like cones of fairy dust. I know Nelson is awake because he hasn't yet started to snore. "How do I please him?"

"If I knew," Nelson murmurs, "I would be doing it myself."

"But he loves you guys," I say. "I'm the one who disappoints him. I can't walk on my hands for fifteen minutes or do a front flip."

"Give yourself a break." Nelson sighs. "Go to sleep."

I think about his words: *Give yourself a break.* These are not words I can comprehend on any level. I can't let up for a minute. So I throw myself at the floor harder, faster, like a pinball ricocheting off walls, bloody and slick with sweat, until Tone, at last, approves of me. "Good," he says. "You are ready for New York."

He delivers a script that showcases our physical training, loosely depicting seven crippled beings (another woman has joined us) navigating their way toward wholeness. The title? *Kaaka-Makaakoo* (Monkey Shit). Tone has a perverse sense of humor, but we are too tired to laugh. Otrabanda Company takes *Monkey Shit* to the La MaMa Theatre in New York, performing for all the avant-garde bigwigs and little wigs alike. Tone has gambled that he could transform seven bumbling college students into acrobatic virtuosos of experimental theater, and it has paid off. The critics rave.

"A panel of Pieter Bruegel come alive!" they write. "The actors are formidable, beyond themselves." Audiences cheer in approval of our groundbreaking new work, *Monkey Shit.* No one is more stunned than we are; we are juggling furniture while belting the choral of Beethoven's Ninth, for God's sake.

But Tone has succeeded, I see now, in peeling back a layer of artifice and revealing the animal beneath our skin. We have learned to move with elemental grace, and we are stripped to the bone. We've been reduced to a luminous expression of primal humanity. What audiences can't see are the scars. Too young to salvage our self-esteem from the brutal dictates of our training, we continue to do what we know best: throwing ourselves against the loveless altar of our art.

I am Somebody at last. There are reviews of Otrabanda in the *Times*, in the *Village Voice*. I write to my dad and tell him to pick up the paper so he can see who I've become. The brief moments when his gaze lands on me are as rare and magical as a unicorn sighting; I bathe in their light. But he is on his way to Finland, and I won't see him this year. Maybe, I fantasize, sadly riffling through my reviews, André Gregory will adopt me and someone can make a movie about our dinner together. "I could live in my art but never in my life," André will confide, deboning his trout with spidery fingers as camera lights blaze around us.

"I know just what you mean," I will say, smugly sipping my ice water. "Daddy."

Tone goes back to Belgium and we launch an East Coast tour. We tour colleges, performing *Monkey Shit* and offering workshops in physical theater as developed by Polish director Jerzy Grotowski. It's the early seventies, and we are the cutting edge. Theater no longer employs curtains or costumes or face paint. The actor's art is muscular physicality, the ability to deploy hundreds of facial muscles to convey emotion, the precisely controlled athletics of gesture.

In the fall, when the tour is over, we move to a farmhouse in southern Vermont to build a new show. But something is missing. While I crave the promise of fame and acceptance, the testosterone-fueled compulsion of my fellow actors generates panic in my bones. I can't keep up. Or maybe I don't want to keep up. I

no longer see the point in throwing myself at walls, juggling furniture, and plunging into ice-cold rivers at dawn. I can't bring
myself to perfect superhuman gymnastic routines far into the
night. I have forgotten the purpose of it all. But the rest of the
troupe has grown little tiny Tones inside of them, and they can
still hear his Gauloises-stinky Belgian yells echoing tinnily inside
their brains as they sleep.

*Harder! Faster! That was shit, Stephen! Use your arms, Roger!
Five more flips, Graham! Ignore the hematoma on your spine.*

I want out.

I don't know then that what I crave in every cell of my being
is not—as I think it is—acceptance by the masculine heroes of
contemporary culture. It is a connection with something deeper,
something I have lost along the way: the ability to trust myself,
to heed my inner urgings. I am a sensitive woman trying to pass
as a man, and the charade has turned me into a salt plain, lifeless
and dry.

As with all cults, it's impossible to leave. They don't cut off
all contact with the outside world or make me drink Kool-Aid.
They don't lock me in my room at night and force me to perform elbow-stands until dawn.

They weep.

"You can't leave, Cynthia," says Stephen, putting down his
juggling pins to gaze into my eyes. "We're a family."

"We've been through so much together." Roger wipes sweat
from his face, gulping water from a canteen. "It would be like
losing a limb."

"Besides, you're just getting good," Graham pipes in, walking
across the room on his hands.

I waffle. We have shared blood, tears, and a small amount of fame, and I have bonded with these intense, sweaty souls. "I don't know what I feel," I try to explain over breakfast. "It's either love," I say, buttering my toast and taking a deep breath, "or Stockholm syndrome."

I plunge into the icy river behind our house after breakfast and fling myself against a few walls before lunch. Later, in bed, I try to talk to Graham about what I am feeling. "I don't know what to do," I say. "I feel empty inside."

"Are you having your period?"

"*No*, I'm not having my period."

"Well, jeez. A guy can ask, can't he?"

The next morning, I flee. "Sorry, guys," I call, waving miserably through the window of my Karmann Ghia. "Something's missing, and I have a sinking feeling that it's me."

I hurtle across the North American continent in my little red car, snorting with grief, aching like an amputee. I have left behind a perfectly good family in a Vermont farmhouse. I worked hard for that family, and I finally belonged. What am I doing? How will I be Someone? I've given up my shot at success, and for what? A mysterious glint of something I can't even name?

My mother is in the States to attend some cousin's wedding (although she never attends her children's weddings), so I drive to Madison and collapse on her hotel bed, hoping against hope for sympathy.

"Get a pedicure," she says.

I'll try Dad, I think.

When I arrive at my dad's house, still trolling for compassion, he says, "Look at the morning glories." This, I must admit, gives me pause.

I guess it's a consider-the-lilies-of-the-field-type remark, but since we have neither lilies nor fields, he's telling me to consider the morning glories that climb in blue abundance across the brick walls of his mock Tudor house. So I consider the morning glories and realize he's telling me to climb out of my head long enough to see the beauty around me. This is useful advice, so I plan a trip to go find beauty somewhere else. I may have missed his point.

My mother gives me money to take a trip far away from whatever ails me, so I book passage on a ship to France, where one of my older sisters resides. I figure I'll sail away and write the great American novel (great novelists never fly), so I pack my typewriter, haul myself aboard, and spend five days playing cutthroat Scrabble with a formidably educated eighty-year-old philosophy professor named Felix.

"You, my dear," says Felix, sliding "QUARTOS" onto the triple-word score for ninety-six points, "can succeed at anything you attempt because you are creative and pretty and a shark at Scrabble."

Why couldn't you be my father? I think. I could swan into my dotage in an orgy of self-esteem.

I don't write a word of the great American novel, though I try, huffing over my dented Smith Corona in my tiny shipboard cabin, Hemingway looming over my shoulder like a disappointed ghost. Everything I write is solipsistic and juvenile, but considering that I *am* a solipsistic juvenile, I'm surprised that

I'm surprised by this. I cover page after page with sorry starts, but no novel emerges. Lack of product notwithstanding, we arrive in France right on schedule.

Traveling from Le Havre to Paris in a second-class train compartment, reading something ostentatious like Nietzsche or Marcuse in case someone is watching, I am bowled over by the disturbing odor of goat. A satyr-like man swirls into my compartment with a whoosh of rank air and plunks himself onto the seat next to me, breathing like a bellows and pressing his thigh into mine. It's impossible to ignore this wild-haired Frenchman coated in sheepskin (which explains the goat). Before I can utter a word, he seizes my Nietzsche and invites me to his apartment, gabbling away about the demise of God. I go home with him. (I have the annoying habit of going home with pretty much anyone who asks.)

The great American novel be damned, I think. Life is to be lived. I spend three days with François in his dungeon apartment in the *quatorzième*, where the ceilings are five feet high and the loo—a hole in the floor—is down the hall behind a cracked, un-lockable door. He takes my mind off my derailed career. He makes me feel precious and important, and he begs me to sail away with him on his charter boat, where I can learn to be as carefree and windswept as he is. However, *windswept* is not in my vocabulary. *Carefree* never made it into my DNA. But he tries. He removes my jewelry one piece at a time in a ritual of despoilment while reading aloud from *Le Petit Prince*. He tries to open my heart through the door of my body. It's hopeless. But François keeps up the siege, making love to me like a pirate while he weeps like a child.

"Cynthia," he says as we lie in his unclean bed. "As I peel off your clothing, imagine that I am peeling away your fears. You American girls understand nothing about love."

He's right. I am twenty-one years old and, despite a few thrashings between the sheets in college, an emotional virgin. I will not recognize the naked face of love until I sit on a river rock with my husband-to-be ten tumultuous years later. Sex, for me, is just a road to acceptance.

We eat dinner at François's Algerian father's Algerian restaurant in the Algerian *quartier*, Papa leering at me as he recounts stories of his exploits as a sailor. We eat with our fingers, drink lots of wine, and field dirty jokes from Papa, who, like a pirate, has a hook for a hand. "Fishing accident," they tell me, winking at one another in dark, Mediterranean collusion. Perhaps a jilted woman hacked it off. Papa dispenses a few more wild tales, and François and I go home to continue my sexual education. I have layers of inhibition, he informs me, ingrained (I suspect) by my mother's early diatribes on the subject of sex.

My mother sat me down when I was a knob-kneed eight-year-old dying to clamber into the safety of my jacaranda tree. My favorite activity was making out with a branch, which I pretended was a prince. But that would have to wait.

Mama wanted to talk.

She sat beside me on the floor in a pool of sunlight and took my hand. One thing I loved about my mother was her hands. They were workman's hands, stout and muscular as fireplugs. She kept her nails short and polished with a clear varnish, and I was proud of those utilitarian mitts that spoke of manual labor and the possibility of demolishing buildings single-handedly.

"Darling," she said, drawing a great breath.

I cringed as the spotlight of her attention swung toward me. I tried to suck myself deep inside my body, hoping to become invisible.

"There is nothing more fabulous," she hissed, "than a man's dick."

"I have to go." I didn't want to have this conversation any more than I wanted to be kidnapped by burglars in the middle of the night. My skin was crawling.

"I must explain this, because how else will you know?" She rearranged her bottom on the parquet floor, rooting in for a long-range assault. "You're almost a woman."

I am? I thought, blindly panicking. *I'm only eight.*

"And this is something every woman has to learn." She lit a cigarette, clearly planning to indulge in the full-length feature version rather than the quickie bulletin I was hoping for. I squirmed in my teddy bear shorts, wishing I could flee.

Waving her cigarette, she continued. "A man isn't good for much, but you need him for sex, so here's the deal: you must massage his ego to get to his dick."

I gagged. I did not want to hear that word—not now, not ever.

"What I want you to know, Cindy darling," she continued, "is that *it's worth it.*"

"But, Mama—" I was planning to tell her that I still played with jump ropes, but she barged ahead.

"Here's the thing." She leaned forward. "It's all a charade.

Marriage is a charade, families are a charade, even love is a great big hoo-ha. It's all about sex, sweetie, and I'm going to tell you how that works."

I bolted out of the sunlight and raced through the door. I was up my tree and clinging to my branch in less than a minute. I didn't want to know how sex worked any more than I wanted the naked rapists from the insane asylum to come to dinner. I clung to my branch and wiped tears from my face. *Oh please*, I thought.

I just wanted to be a child.

François is an avid teacher, but I mope around Paris with a baffling sense of aimlessness. I try to submerge my overstimulated sensibilities in the sensuous worlds of D. H. Lawrence and Henry Miller, and I discard multiple pages of rumpled novel starts. If I can't tolerate the self-flagellation of the theater and I'm not going to write the great American novel, how on earth will I become Someone? It's the first of many cycles of manic aspiration followed by bewildered withdrawal.

Bewildered and withdrawn, I stumble along the banks of the Seine, wondering what trajectory my dislocated life will take now. Someday, perhaps, I will go back to the theater, but in the meantime, I decide to return to the safest haven of all, home of irrelevant theories, outdated tautologies, and uneventful intimacies: school.

When in doubt, go back to school. Choose oversized brick buildings, smothered in hundred-year-old ivy, where you can study things you'll never need to know, write papers on subjects you have no interest in, and prove points that will help humanity absolutely never. Do all this assiduously, and you can quell the voices of existential doubt for one more year. Do it long enough, and they'll give you a piece of paper that says you've earned the right to venture forth into the predatory world of commerce and enterprise.

You will have a bachelor of arts degree. Even though your degree may have nothing to do with bachelors of any kind (except the number you've bedded while studying) and less to do with art, it will represent, certainly, a degree. To *a degree*, you will be ready for the world. With a bachelor of arts degree, you will be more or less qualified to do nothing.

I earn a bachelor of arts degree in, of all the unremunerative vocations available to me, theater.

CHAPTER THREE

Hungry for Love and Blind to Its Sticker Price

I GRADUATE FROM COLLEGE IN 1973 AND PUT A SIGN ON the University of Wisconsin bulletin board: *Wanted: inspiring and creative fellow traveler to San Francisco, willing to share driving and expenses.* With my theater degree in hand, I am moving to California, land of hot tubs and honey. Land of hippies and surfers and rock music in the streets, land of lost souls and plenty of pot(s) to find them under.

Stallion calls.

"Your name is *Stallion?*" I warble, imagining a misplaced cowpoke in chaps and a Stetson wandering the Wisconsin corn-fields with only a harmonica to his name. I get the harmonica part right. Throw in a guitar, a shredded backpack, and a pound of killer marijuana, and you've got Stallion.

"Do you have a last name?" I pray.

"No."

That should be warning enough right there, but oh no, not for me. I like the slippery slopes of borderline psychos with guitar cases and no last names. They remind me that I'm not my mother.

"I call myself Stallion," he intones in a mellow voice that

oozes into my ear canal like a greased snake, "because I want to change everything about myself, to reprogram my childhood conditioning and reinvent myself as a powerful avatar. I'm a musician," he adds.

I should stop the conversation right here. Anyone in their right mind would be alert to the disasters and errors in judgment that will ensue from associating with a spurious dude with a name like Stallion. Not me. I'm on the lookout for some new kind of initiation, one that will imbue me with the elusive qualities I obviously lack.

Discernment is not my strong suit.

My excuse for sleeping with Stallion is the freak snowstorm that forces the Karmann Ghia into a 180-degree spin in the middle of Nebraska. While I sit there, breathing hard, facing the headlights of oncoming traffic, Stallion says in his honeyed voice, "Let's get a room."

Sharing a room is the first but not the last error in judgment that will come to litter my feral relationship with Stallion No-Last-Name, the musician. I am hungry for love and blind to its sticker price. It will be years before I learn the word *no*.

The dude, I have to admit, is not easy on the eyes: he has the face of a ferret. But driving across the plains, he plays beautiful music and plies me with grass strong enough to fell an elephant, and I am able to overlook his lack of chin. Right up until we flip on the searing fluorescent light of that interstate motel room. I stare with dismay, but Stallion lights another joint and pulls out his guitar.

Here's the thing. He has an uncanny ability to shape-shift like a genie. With enough THC of the brain-warping variety, which he keeps readily available, he can make himself look as divinely sexy as Krishna ogling Radha. How does he do that? *He sings.*

When he sings, his homeliness dissolves. You melt into deep auditory bliss. Before you know it, you're tearing your clothes off to mount the little gnome, regardless of whether his teeth are crooked (they are) or his frame is skinny (it is). It's only when the sunlight pours through the Dacron drapes that you gasp once again. *This guy's a real dog! What am I* thinking?

Stallion has his act down. Guitar at the ready, joint lit, drapes drawn—it gets him laid on a regular basis.

By the time we reach San Francisco, my city of choice on the Left Coast, Stallion has me convinced that (1) he's beautiful, (2) he's a brilliant musician (he may be, but I never get off his pot long enough to make an objective assessment), and (3) his two girlfriends—*yes, two*—will come out and live with us while I support them all with my little trust fund.

Apparently the first girlfriend is still getting used to the second girlfriend's presence; the first girlfriend had been hoping for a nice middle-class wedding with her high school sweetheart, Bobby, when the second girlfriend came along and transformed Bobby into Stallion, genius mastermind of a free-sex commune. First girlfriend threw a hissy fit, which Stallion dismissed as bourgeois before demanding that she jump into bed with second girlfriend.

"Wait until Melissa licks *your* toes," Stallion promises me, and in a haze of cannabis delirium, I agree to let Melissa lick my toes. It's somewhat incriminating that I haven't even met Melissa, but I am once again up to my chin cleft in extreme behavior, willing to sign over my grandparents' trust fund to three people I don't know.

"Hi, Mr. Carson," I say when I call my banker, the guy in charge of the previously mentioned trust fund, otherwise known as Mama's flunky. "It's Cynthia Moore. Can you wire all my funds to this bank in California? I'm forming a commune."

Jon Carson, bless his soul, does not miss a beat. "I'll see what I can do, Cynthia. How's the weather out there?"

My mother flies out on the next plane.

She never comes stateside for weddings, graduations, or any of those meaningful rites of passage that entice a normal mother, but she pops right over for this.

By the time she arrives, Stallion's first and second girlfriends have arrived in San Francisco and we've set ourselves up in an apartment on the corner of Haight and Ashbury—*I kid you not*—adding to our commune a truly fine African American jazz musician whose name I won't mention because he would sue me in a New York minute.

My mother invites us to dinner at the Mark Hopkins, and we decide that only Melissa will accompany me because she's the most presentable of our little group. Melissa, in a gypsy skirt and low-cut top, is barefoot. I, praying that this collision between my two worlds will not result in nuclear fission, wear a dress I dug out from the back of my closet. The maître d' glances at Melissa's bare feet, then at my mother's high-shine Gucci loafers, and sails without a backward glance to the far corner of the restaurant, where he plunks us in shadowy oblivion.

"What the hell are you thinking?" my mother asks without preamble.

Melissa, as previously agreed, takes the lead. "We don't agree with the fascist hypocrisy of the corporate culture. We value art and free love. You can't stop us."

Well, of course my mother can stop us—*that's the whole point of a trust fund, dummy*—but I don't know that yet. We are revolutionaries, carving out glorious new standards in a corrupt society. We believe in Total Honesty, Free Love, Sex for All, and Communal Sharing. We're saving the world by breaking its taboos. Melissa is *barefoot* at the Mark Hopkins, for God's sake.

"You're out of your minds," says my mother, buttering her bread with her gorgeous, clunky hands. "Of course I can stop you, and I *will* stop you, you can be certain of that, but let's have a nice talk about it first so at least you won't go home feeling infantilized."

My mother's take-no-prisoners pragmatism floors even the mellifluous Melissa. Melissa has met her match. Her ravishing bisexual beauty has no effect on this woman, and she isn't used to feeling ineffectual. Her jaw hangs open in an unattractive leer. I gently reach over and close it.

"First of all," Mom says, popping a ladylike crust of bread into her mouth, "who will take care of you when you get old and sick if you give away all your money?" This offensive *sortie* is directed at me, her eyes drilling into my brain like twin lasers.

"We're going to get jobs," I whine. "We don't need handouts from you." *Infantilized.*

"Maybe not now," she snaps. "But when you're seventy and you get cancer and it costs thousands of dollars to get the care you need, where will you get that kind of money?"

I am opening my mouth to answer this appallingly morbid prediction when she suddenly changes tack. Oh, she's smart, my mother. She has always been smarter than me.

"What about when *I* need emergency care? You won't want to welcome me into your little commune and take care of me until I die. How will you afford to hire the round-the-clock medical personnel that *I* will need?"

She has me. I'm willing to starve, to become destitute, uninsured, and sick, but I'm not willing to take my mother home with me. Suddenly, I'm not hungry. The waiter delivers my scallops and risotto, a mountain of calories in butter-cream perfection, and I can barely swallow. I want to go home to my hippie haven in the Haight.

Mama, for all her sexual compulsions and innate broken-ness, is like Mount Rushmore that night: absolute power carved from sheer granite. She is inexorable. My money is cut off.

Melissa and I manage to gobble our *crème brûlée* without further humiliation. My mother spends the rest of the meal entertaining us with anecdotes about my stepfather's poodle.

"She loves *pommes frites*," she chortles. "Howard lets her eat off his plate." She titters, forking up her *tarte aux poires*. "Dog's mouths," she informs me with an accusing eye, "are *much* cleaner than yours."

I roll my eyes.

Swearing she isn't jealous of the spoiled-rotten pom-pom of canine fluff, Mom applies a perfect coat of French Cherry by Dior to her smacking lips, signs the check with a flourish, and sails out of the restaurant, her mission, as always, accomplished.

The enterprising enthusiasm of our Haight-Ashbury commune dims at the specter of penury. We're running out of money. This leads to increased bickering among the females and diminished experimental verve among the males. Who will buy supper? How many more nights can we survive on canned mackerel?

We girls accompany Stallion to his auditions with music producers, each of which, he swears, will bring the breakthrough he desires. Decades later, I'll realize how closely we resemble Charlie Manson's coterie, waltzing stoned into Marin County ranch houses and grinning vacuously while Stallion plays. But at the time, we believe he's an undiscovered genius. *Why do girls glue themselves to narcissists?* We so badly want to believe in something more vibrant than the Vietnam War, the Kent State pigs, and the military-industrial complex. We're young and clever and clueless, and we want to subvert the dominant culture. We dance and make theater; we resist the war by lying in the streets; we shut down military bases and are carted off to prison. We bail each other out so we can go back to the streets and shout slogans until we're hoarse. It's the era of the Black Panthers and women's liberation. The world of old white guys is fracturing (we hope). We want to pry off the masks of greed and fakery and plant the seeds of authentic artistry.

To this end, Melissa and I spend an afternoon leaping about the meadows of Golden Gate Park in a frenzy of self-expression. While we are cavorting, a police cruiser pulls up to the curb. A boxy black-and-white sedan disgorges a Tyranno-saurus rex of a cop, who emerges swinging a club, swaying meaningfully across the grass as if he's on a mission to save the free world.

"What do you think you're doing?" he growls.

Melissa and I glance at each other, surprised because on this rarest of occasions, we are not actually performing an illegal act. "Dancing," we reply, adopting bland, doe-eyed expressions.

"Doesn't look like any kind of dancing I've ever seen," Dinosaur-cop intones.

"Then you've been deprived," chirps Melissa, twirling about in a tour jeté.

"What are you girls on?" he barks, slamming his stick against the ham of his hand. "Acid?"

We stare at the man, our mouths agape. We have ingested plenty of acid, but today we are not on anything at all. It strikes us as absurd that we should be arrested for dancing. We tumble on the grass in a heap of laughter. Dinosaur-cop is not amused.

"You're coming with me," he says, reaching out a calloused paw.

We stop laughing.

"Let's go." His gun belt creaks as he approaches us.

We don't want to go to jail. We are only twenty-two. We want our mommies. "Please, Mister Officer Sir, we are only dancing. We are not on drugs—you can look in our eyes. We are high on life, sir. It's not a crime," Melissa pleads.

I am trying not to cry. *High on life*, I think. *That's a good one.*

"Don't let me catch you doing this again," he mutters, swinging around and heading back toward his patrol car. "Freaks."

We stand shrunken and dejected in the field where we twirled, only minutes ago, in ecstatic satisfaction. This, we think to ourselves, is a snapshot of 1974: cops against flower children, uniformed dinosaurs stamping regulation work boots on the tender young chicklings of the Love Generation.

We can barely pay our rent.

The only fully employed member of our commune is our unnamed jazz musician, X. X is a sensual saxophonist who can raise the hairs on your arms with his high C, and he skitters in and out of the apartment at strange hours, glancing fearfully into the kitchen where there's always a domestic squabble unfolding between Stallion's "women." The claustrophobia of spending all our time together, in addition to our increased lack of income, is making us cranky. We eschew jealousy and other bourgeois emotions, but that doesn't stop us from ripping each other's hair out over who used the last of the jalapeño jack.

I have a part-time job teaching drama to kids, and with the little money I make, I decide to take an acting class in Berkeley. It's my first foray into theater since I left Otrabanda, and I feel as skittish as a chicken on a conveyor belt. But when I arrive at the cinderblock studio bedecked with ferns and sunny skylights, I am relieved to see that, instead of throwing ourselves at the walls, we are invited to sit in a circle and share our feelings.

"Our feelings must inform our performance," the lanky, androgynous teacher drones as he strolls through the studio undressing his female students with limpid eyes. "We have to find our *authenticity* in order to inhabit the stage. Otherwise, we are mere personas, *frauds*, disconnected from our true selves."

I am spellbound. I will not be required to perform a front flip. I exhale, lean back on my hands, and prepare to surrender my false self.

"What are our true selves?" he asks, leering at each of us in turn, six nubile young women and one terrified young man. When we gaze at him with our mouths falling open, he shouts, "Our *wounds!*"

I gasp. No one has ever referred to my wounds. It feels sexual, as though he's prodding my labia. My blood pulses. *I could be good at exposing my wounds*, I think.

"We must rip away the bandages that hide our *pain*, and we must *expose* it to the public eye," he continues. I'm overheating. "What is the one thing we are most afraid of?" He glares at us. "Cynthia?"

"Uh . . . failure?" I venture.

"NO! Exposing our *pain*." He strides purposefully around the tiny studio, gesticulating, performing the role of drama magnate with unbridled gusto. "We are so afraid that our *wounds* will be exposed that we scurry and hide even from ourselves. The audience sees nothing but a *persona*, masking a true soul beneath a false exterior. The audience sees right through that exterior. They don't want artifice. They want *truth*."

I lean toward him like a plant reaching for the sun. *Peel me back*, I pray. *Make me real.*

Naturally, I sleep with him. Lying on a lumpy futon on the floor of his studio, I silently enumerate my fervent hopes: I will expose my wounds; I will be purged, cleansed, and made authentic; and last but not least, I will get the lead role in his play.

Stallion doesn't share my enthusiasm.

Apparently, the bourgeois jealousy responses forbidden to women are allowed to men. The night I dare to bring the Drama Magnate home to my Haight-Ashbury mattress, Stallion crashes into my room, cursing. Drama Magnate scurries home, and the next morning, I enter the kitchen to find all six of my potted plants smashed in a carnage of exposed roots.

My illusions fall away. We have been riding high on clouds of Thai stick, imagining a Utopian world of love and sharing that we are incapable of embodying. We are just as greedy and competitive as the corporate-industrial patriarchy that we despise. I look at those shattered plants on the floor, and I see the truth: I have—once again—sought love in the wrong places. The price of belonging is too high.

I move out.

Shuddering and fragile, I crash on my friend Susie's couch in Oakland, swearing I will never speak to Stallion or his twisted mistresses again. Melissa, I hear, replaces me in the Drama Magnate's bed within a week.

I can't face the wreckage of my life, so I find someone to teach my drama classes and I flee, in another phase of bewildered withdrawal, to Hawaii.

Airports will always have, for me, a blurry patina of hope. The brand-new possibilities, the opening of gates. Escape. I willingly confess: I have a tendency to extricate myself from painful situations by leaving town. Planes are great. And now that I have jettisoned my free-love commune, I have renewed access to my trust fund.

I step off the plane in Oahu into blissfully humid air that melts my worries. Drunk on the scent of plumeria, I heft my backpack and hitchhike to a friend's house in Haleiwa. I have to find work. Soon I am performing with a Honolulu theater troupe and working at a North Shore preschool. No more cults. No more sacrifices on the altar of dysfunctional love.

In Hawaii, I discover that I live on a planet of exceptional beauty, and I surrender to the hot, wild embrace of nature.

I have the best education money can buy, I have endless opportunities, and, purely by accident, I end up in the one place on earth that can teach me what I really need to know. (Sometimes you've got to wonder who's planning all this.)

I am walking the beach at Haena when a ten-year-old girl dives into the sea. Shading my eyes, I watch a giant wave crash over her head. I wait an endless minute, but she doesn't come up for air. Without thinking, I plunge in. I remember a Vietnam medic telling me about the biological urge that propelled him into near-death rescue situations. "It's an impulse so primal," he said, "it bypasses thought." I am halfway to the girl before I have my first inkling: *This might be a bad idea.*

By the time I reach her, the waves are pounding me into the ocean floor. I shove her skyward, hoping to launch her toward the shore, but the crashing surf tumbles me in a spin cycle, and I can no longer tell which way is up. The undertow has me in its teeth, and when I finally manage to thrust her to the surface, I find myself upside-down and panicking. A man swims out and seizes the girl, and before I can thank him, I am sucked under again, roiling in the riptide. When I emerge, hacking and sputtering, the next wave slams me harder. I've inhaled half the ocean. I spin like wet laundry, tossed by a force so primal it doesn't care if I've been a good Catholic or a bad actor. Whatever I am, I'm gonna be dead.

This is it. I try to scream, and fifty gallons of water pour down my throat. I choke on the tsunami, and then I suddenly stop struggling; I realize that whatever I am fighting is so much huger than anything I've ever encountered, I will never win. There's no point in trying.

I'm going—flipping head over heels, I cry redundant salty tears—*to die.* My muscles turn to liquid and the waves break my will. That's when I give up. I say goodbye to my body and *sayonara* to my life and farewell to my friends and family, and grief strikes me so hard that my heart cracks. *I haven't even begun to live!*

Just as I'm about to sink like a stone, the ocean picks me up and tosses me toward shore. At the precise moment that I surrender my will, she sweeps me up in her great fishy arms and dumps me in the shallows. When my feet find solid sand, I inhale a delicious lungful of air and yell. In that instant, with people on the beach applauding, I realize that, instead of devouring me whole and spitting out my masticated bones in an orgy of divine retribution, the ocean has saved me.

"Dude," I say. "What just happened?"

You stopped struggling.

The playground monitor is back.

It's the first clue I've ever had that I can't win by trying.

I think of the Zen monk who wanders the ranks of feverish meditators with a two-by-four to slam into their heads when he senses they are sliding back into the illusion that they are in charge. We are not in charge of any of this.

I have always entertained the illusion that I am in charge. I survived boarding school and got through college. I bought a car, rented an apartment, got disillusioned, flew to Hawaii. I seek one agent of change after another, hoping always to heal something, to repair something I secretly imagine is broken.

But what if it isn't broken? What if all our attempts to improve ourselves, to attain something, to manipulate reality, are a waste of time? What if there is nothing to do but surrender? *Shut up and pay attention*, my playground monitor whispered so long ago.

It's my first encounter with a reality far bigger than the one inside my own skull. I decide that if the directive is to surrender, I might as well surrender to the path I started on in the first place, because if it isn't the right path, I'll get picked up and tossed onto another path just like I was picked up and tossed onto the shore in Hawaii. First I'll drown and choke on some seaweed, then I'll stop struggling and will be delivered to some unforeseen beach where the gulls are whiter than bleached sheets and the sun is blazing into my eyes to remind me that my path is simply the one I'm already on.

I return to the Bay Area to make theater.

CHAPTER FOUR

Not Bad for a Girl

SAN FRANCISCO IS THE MECCA OF LEARNING. YOU CAN LEARN anything in San Francisco, from reading tarot cards to performing astral clearings for cats. There are universities that teach "The 40-Minute Orgasm" and professional chakra cleaners who sweep your system squeaky clean in under twelve seconds. I am teaching drama to schoolchildren, exhorting ten-year-olds to learn sharp comedic timing and physical character acting while trying to find work in the theater. I have to believe that my gift of hurling myself against walls is marketable; I just need to find the right market.

It turns out that there is a troupe of actors in Berkeley who are trained in the same kind of Grotowski-esque physical theater. Although America still prefers the Wonder Bread school of entertainment (bland, mealy, traditional), European theater is harsh, frightening, and risky. Poor Theater, Grotowski calls it, because with highly trained actors, expensive sets and follow spots are no longer required. A single actor balanced on his index finger in a bare room is all that is needed for pure expression. Poor Theater signifies a return to the human body, a re-sacralizing of the physical form so profound that the actor's body becomes translucent in its expression. Physically trained actors have the musculature of dancers and the flexibility of acrobats. It is theater in its purest form.

Still searching for a home, I trot off to a grungy warehouse behind a Plexiglas factory and find myself face-to-face with four unwashed males staring at my breasts. Predictably, it's an all-male club. It's misguided, it's problematic, it's all too familiar. *But I want in.* The urge to belong pulses in my belly like cholera.

"We trained in Iowa," they say, as if that should scare the whimpers out of me. "No one does what we do."

The hackles (what *are* hackles, anyway?) lift on the back of my neck, and I peer around the dusty cave where they work. It hasn't been painted or even cleaned in years, from the looks of it. They may sorely need a woman's touch, but what they need even more is a tongue-lashing.

"Are you referring to kips, flips, cradles, and *plastiques*?" I ask coolly. "Because *I* trained with Grotowski's Dutch cousin's brother-in-law."

My training was (I reckon) more purebred than theirs, and they don't appreciate the insinuation. "Okay, you can work with us," one of them grumbles. "For one week. We'll see if you can keep up."

"Done."

These fellows need to learn a lesson. If they think they're the only slugs in America who can hit a wall with aplomb, they'll be eating their Sheetrock by Friday.

Hit the wall we do, repeatedly, viciously, and with double-barreled machismo blazing. Tone would be proud of me. I'm no longer vanilla pudding. I'm a double chocolate mocha fudge torte with nuts, and these boys want a bite of me.

"Not bad," they grudgingly allow as the week draws to an end. "For a girl."

I swell with pride and join the Blake Street Hawkeyes, officially becoming one of the guys. I fling myself across the room, perform insane acrobatic feats, and chain-smoke cigarettes while cursing like a back-alley pimp. It's exhilarating. I have become a force to be reckoned with. I've become a man.

At first, I speak up for myself. "You think all women are either whores or nuns," I tell John. "I'm more than that. Show some respect." Brimming with hope, I clean the studio, wash the windows, and buy colorful cushions for our floor-seated audiences.

I teach the men ballet, hiding my smirk as they pirouette clumsily across the floor, and they teach me martial arts and tumbling. Dripping with sweat, we train for eight hours a day, and our bodies are lean and muscled. I feel powerful and alive for the first time in years.

These days of jazz improvisation and physical playfulness are the freest, the wildest, the most unconstrained of my life, but every day, I secretly compare myself to the men. They are bigger and brighter. They are icons of unrepressed masculine energy. They are spontaneous and funny. If testosterone expresses itself as the incandescence of a noonday sun, I am a silvery moon hunting for a source of light. I belong to this group of hairy primates, but what is my role?

There was, before me, one other woman in the troupe (her name was Deb). She sensibly retired to the hills of Vermont. Audiences and critics laud me for her past performances and call me by her name. When she returns years later, they will credit her with my performances and call her by my name. We are, in this all-male tribe, a symbol of something, but we don't know what it is.

I don't want to know.

Take my very first performance as a Hawkeye. The troupe hosts three-day Actualist Conventions, a compilation of wild, mismatched performances by dozens of poets, dancers, musicians, and theater artists. A cultlike fervor surrounds these events; performance artists jostle for space in the dimly lit hallway. The Hawkeyes are going to perform a piece that introduces their newest member (*moi*) to their fans. It's a hip-rolling burlesque called *Big Peen*, and it's sung to the tune of "Heartbreak Hotel."

It's a show about their penises.

The heartbreak for me is that I participate, thrusting my pelvis and declaiming the size of my (whatever). It might be funny were I not so oblivious, but probably, as with most shows we'll do together over the years, no one notices my discomfort as I punch my hips and sing loudly about the largesse of my peen.

It's the seventies, and feminism insists that women are as powerful as men, but I mishear the message as *Women are powerful when men give them permission.*

Holy hell.

"Let's make a list show," says George, mopping the floor before rehearsal.

"What's a list show?" The rest of us are engaged in random avoidant behaviors such as changing our clothes, stretching our hamstrings, or making a third trip to the bathroom. This is not because we don't want to rehearse but because jumping into the creative void requires serious procrastination.

"It's a show," explains George, wringing the wet mop into an industrial-sized bucket, "made up of unrelated events like a drumming call/response section, an acrobatic sequence, and some soap opera dialogue superimposed on an environmental performance piece, with a few sociopolitical monologues sprinkled into some inexplicable dry humping. We throw them all together with no apparent connective tissue and the audience makes meaning."

"Why don't we make our own meaning? I want to do a piece about sex," says Bob. "Call it *Tantrums*."

"A list piece would be more interesting," insists George. "We trick the audience, see? They think there's meaning to our anarchy—they pray there's meaning because nobody can tolerate anarchy for more than a minute, so they invent the meaning they want to see." He rolls the bucket into the back room and reappears like a rabbit from a magician's hat.

"Maybe," we say.

It's an intriguing idea. We're always trying to shock, awaken, or clobber our audience with a new and unexpected performance idea. Anything but the old "neck-up" theater in which actors stand around stiff as boards, belting their lines with bad British accents. We want to smash the old and usher in the new.

We *are* the new. We are funded by the state of California to define *cutting edge*.

Two hours later, while practicing backflips on the floor mat, George grabs his sternum. "I'm having chest pains," he groans. The rest of us stop leaping long enough to stare at him. *Chest pains?*

He's twenty-eight.

George doubles over and falls to his knees. "I can't breathe," he gasps.

Of course, we've just smoked some highly illegal substance to facilitate the emergence of our incipient creativity, and we're unsure of what—in reality—we are supposed to do. We're stoned out of our minds.

"I think I'm having a heart attack," George mumbles, curling up in a fetal position on the floor. This strikes the fear of God into us. We fly into action, going in four directions at once, babbling incoherently.

"Call 911."

"Do you have a doctor, George? What's his number?"

"Call his girlfriend."

"We should call someone."

"Call his mother!"

Panting, we stare at George's body on the floor.

"Call an ambulance, for God's sake," gabbles George, digging his chin into his chest. He wheezes dramatically.

These are the days before cell phones, so someone has to go and find a fifty-pound phone attached to a wall somewhere, which is easier said than done in an industrial warehouse on a back street in Berkeley, California, at eleven o'clock at night. "I'll go," says Dave. By this time, we're all having panicky thoughts of losing George before the ambulance can arrive, visions of his dead body sprawled on our freshly mopped floor, images of our canceled show, George's distraught girlfriend, his parents, our parents—*Oh my God*, we think. *He could really die!* In the stupor of my altered state, I glimpse the possibility of real tragedy, and my eyes fill with tears. "George," I say, "Hang on, okay?"

"Just kidding," he says.

There is a silence so thick you could cut it with a chain saw. I take a breath, steadying myself. "What do you mean, 'Just kidding'?"

"I wanted to see what you would do."

George loves to play games. He simulated a heart attack at eleven o'clock at night to see what we would do. *Or maybe it really was a heart attack, and he wanted to see what we would do with that.* We no longer know what's real and what's false.

He grins his infuriating cat-ate-the-goldfish grin and stands up, brushing off his sweatpants. "You'll never know, will you?"

We gape at him, aching at the same time to throttle him and to raise him over our heads for pulling the greatest con in Hawkeye history. "You asshole!" we yell. We chase him around the studio as he skips, nimble as a bee, from one wall to the other. "What a jerk," we chorus.

Exhausted from George's questionable near-death experience, we sit down and make a random list of unrelated activities. Six weeks later, we perform our list show. We ride in on motorcycles, pile ourselves into a pyramid, sing primitive songs, spout random lines of absurdist dialogue, and dance as if our pants are on fire. Then we disappear through a trap door in the roof, reappearing moments later to sing a rousing drum-accompanied chant of "Keep Us Alive!"

The critics surpass themselves with Freudio-Nietzschean interpretations of our mismatched scenes. They extol our intellectual depth and emotional complexity while contorting themselves to discover the existential meaning in our "daring feat of theatrical pyrotechnics." We are the darlings of the avant-garde. We pretend to excavate meaning from cracks in the sidewalk where there is no meaning. But the joke's on us: there's always meaning, even when you're trying so very hard to be a nihilist.

There's a little truth in every lie.

During the next fourteen years, I will mother those crazy primates, fly through the air with them, win awards with them, and pay their dental bills.

I am one of the guys (I think). I yell obscenities, master impossible feats, and take part in tasteless sexist jokes. I share in the steady flow of adulation from fans who are goggle-eyed at the audacity of the risks we take while performing on rooftops and in parking lots, naked and clothed, portraying junkies and transsexuals, whores and cons, preachers and gurus and animals and shamans. We howl, flip through the air, drum till our hearts split, break all the rules that have ever been made, and forge new ones out of jazz, visual anarchy, and bodies that forswear the laws of gravity. We are the front-runners of a glorious, hedonistic, insanely creative era in the theater.

But something is missing.

"Teach me to be myself," I beg John one day. John is the genius of the troupe, and I hope some of his brilliance might rub off on me.

We stand barefoot in the dusty studio as afternoon light streams through the window and pools on the wooden floor. John throws me a puzzled look. The guys have no trouble being themselves. They are pure expressions of physical urgency. I, on the other hand, am "the woman," and what the hell is that?

John scrutinizes me, scratching his uncombed head. "Well," he says, circling me as if I'm a horse for sale, "you have to start by holding something in. You can't give it all away, Cynthia. You have to leave the audience wanting something."

I have no idea what he's talking about. "Show me."

"Just move," he says. "Start moving, and I'll give you directions as you go."

I jump and leap and twirl as I have been so well trained to do. *Look at me*, my movements cry. *Look what I can do.* All the years of competing with men have made me a mini-man. Testosterone is my currency of choice.

"No, no, no," John mutters, scratching his stubbly jaw. "You're too concerned with performing. Close your eyes."

"Close my eyes?"

"Yeah, close your eyes and just be yourself."

I'm flummoxed. I don't know how to "be myself." *What* self?

But I do as I'm told: I close my eyes and continue to leap around the room, flailing my arms.

"What's going on?" John asks. "*Inside* you?"

This only makes me flail harder and leap higher. I am desperate to succeed. *Oh, please*—I pray—*Let me get this right.* In an enormous outburst of bravado, I hurl myself across the room and, with my eyes closed, crash headfirst into a cinderblock wall, collapsing to the floor in a heap.

"Jesus!" John says. "You didn't have to go *that* far."

I open my eyes and stare at him with a drumbeat pounding in my head. The drum in my head intones, *Oh but I did, oh but I did, oh but I really did.* Because that is the only way I know how to be myself. By smashing headfirst into a concrete wall in an excruciating effort to shine.

CHAPTER FIVE

So Much for Feminism

SPONSORED BY THE CALIFORNIA ARTS COUNCIL, THE Blake Street Hawkeyes tour our play *Angel Window/Devil Door* to colleges and universities. The show is essentially a revivalist meeting with witchy voodoo overtones and extraneous scenes of domestic violence: a mismatched amalgam of *Wise Blood* and occult ritual accompanied by Bob on his congas. When we arrive at Monterey Peninsula College's theater building, the door is locked.

We're used to this kind of thing.

We manage to round up a janitor to unlock the door, but the tech and lighting designers are nowhere in sight. Also, the theater department has failed to publicize the event, so no one comes to our show. Actually, one guy stumbles in at eight fifteen, reeking of beer. I call the California Arts Council (which is subsidizing our tour) in a panic and blurt into the phone, "There's only one person in the audience. You can't expect us to do this whole show for one person!"

"Please leave a message," says the recording.

We do the show for our one inebriated customer, who sits

stone-still (if not stone-cold sober) and possibly fast asleep during the entire enterprise. We sing and drum and tear one another's clothes off while exorcising fundamentalist demons. It's a testament to our voracious powers of concentration that we're able to spread our wings and soar into newfound theatrical ecstasies in spite of the motionless lump in the front row. When the house lights go up, his dutiful clapping echoes amid the dust motes and we clunk back to earth, blinking into the merciless glare. Feeling sorry for the poor guy, we take him out for a drink.

"Today I realized," he tells us, slurping his fourth beer, "that I'm gay." He sets his glass down, struggling not to miss the table. "So I had to break up with my girlfriend."

"You broke up with your girlfriend *tonight*?" we chorus.

"Yeah," he burps politely. "Right before your show. That's why I came to the theater." He wipes his mouth with a paper napkin. "I go there to be alone." He adds in apology, "It's usually empty."

We stare at him. "And instead, you had to watch us tear off Velcro clown suits, beat each other up with rubber chickens, and pretend to rise from the dead?"

"It was okay. I didn't *mind*." We buy him another beer.

These are the indignities we put up with as artists while we tear our hearts open onstage.

"Let's do solo shows," Bob suggests as we slog into our studio carrying cardboard cups of lukewarm coffee and all the fervor of exorcists at a demon convention. Stepping into any studio, whether to rehearse or dance or sing, disturbs the little gremlins of doubt and despair, scattering them across the floor like cockroaches. The trick is to plow right through them, pretend they're not there, and get to work even as they nip at your ankles and hiss in your ears. They dissolve once you get to work, but surviving the twenty minutes required to overcome their gummy web is an act of pure faith. Every artist knows these twenty minutes: it's the drooling maw of creation.

What's the point of all this? you ask (feeling sorry for yourself).

The world won't understand anyway.

I'm no good. (That goblin heads straight for your heart, brandishing a knife and fork.)

But we stream in, turn on the lights, mop the floor, bitch and moan, change into our workout clothes, and get to work, starting with floor stretches to warm up.

"We could," continues Bob, "each do a solo show and call it a series." He recently gained notoriety for his marathon twenty-four-hour solo show, during which audience members came and went, slept in sleeping bags, and watched him descend into exhaustion as he continued to sing and drum until the sun rose.

The solo show craze will become rampant in a year or two thanks to Bob and our latest addition to the Hawkeyes who is another woman, *thank God*. A solo show is a form in which theater can be made for very little money in tiny spaces with no overhead. Is it any surprise that soon *every actor* will be performing one?

"Do we have to?" I wail, never having done (shame courses

through my veins) a solo show. I'm afraid I might have nothing to say.

"*Yes*," the others cry, envisioning their names in lights, uncluttered by any other names, and their very own box office take of—oh, maybe $80 per night—fattening their anorexic wallets. In the end, I agree to do a solo show, which I call *If You Lived Here You'd Be Home by Now.*

If I lived anywhere in the vicinity of my own body, I might be home at the ripe old age of thirty-one, but the meaning of *Be Here Now* has not yet dawned on me; I'm too busy trying to *Get There Soon.* I'm still throwing myself at walls and screeching impressions of a hyena in heat, as if exhaustion and overexertion are the sticky criteria of success. In my solo show, I sing Linda Ronstadt tunes while dandling a flashlight under my chin as I huddle inside a refrigerator in a housecoat. Meanwhile, our newest Hawkeye is whisked off to Broadway to perform *her* solo show under the direction of Mike Nichols. (Her wallet, by the way, will soon be fatter than Madonna's ego.)

We hear stories of the star being discovered, swept away in a Lincoln Town Car, and stuffed to the teeth in a five-star restaurant before performing to sold-out crowds at the Lyceum and being touted as "the new Lily Tomlin, only funnier." I wish it were my story, the story in which I become Somebody and impress my dad at last. But it isn't, and I content myself with throwing tomato soup at a black-and-white TV set while singing country-western songs to a pig. I welcome the thirty-three people perched on uncomfortable chairs while I hang upside down and sing "Desperado." It's my story, and I perform it with gusto. That's the thing about solo shows: you can't do someone else's.

It is the first time I perform my own work, and I feel terrified and brave. I am starting to individuate from my man-club.

When Deb (the actress who played "the woman" in Hawkeye shows before I came along) returns to the troupe from the underbrush of Vermont, I recognize her at once even though I have never actually met her.

She is me.

Not only do we look alike, we both have a gymnastic androgyny that denies our breasts and curves and abets us in our attempts to "pass" as guys. We wear men's hats, heavy boots, men's blazers with the cuffs rolled back. We smoke like chimneys and curse like stevedores. We roll on the floor with men, haul them around on our backs, meet them with hard-cracking humor, and shout in their faces. We jump as high, run as fast, and yell as loud as any man.

Why do we sneak off to a darkened bar to talk, as if we have a secret?

"I'm reading some strange books," I tell Deb, lighting a cigarette. We are both on our third glass of wine, having reached the point when conversations become murky and shadowed with secret longings and the incomprehensible tinge of regret. "Virginia Woolf, Edith Wharton," I whisper.

"*Women* writers?"

We shudder. The coiled snakes of mistrust and misgivings lie underneath the word *women*: Eve in the garden exposed as a miscreant while everyone knows that perfect, studly Adam would never have been caught chatting up a snake. Terrified of exposing ourselves, and too brainwashed to know it, we order more wine and take each other's measure. "I don't trust women," I say in my most guttural voice.

"Me neither," Deb growls.

"At least we're agreed on that."

We scan one another's faces. This terrain is littered with shoals of betrayal as our success is most definitely hitched to a masculine star. Women writers and their pallid simpering hold no interest for us. *No, sir.*

Still, I check out books from the library, slipping them into brown paper bags like pornography, glancing over my shoulder to make sure I'm not observed: Colette, Anaïs Nin, Doris Lessing.

"There's something about these books that intrigues me," I confess, gulping my wine, appraising fellow bar hounds to make sure we can't be overheard. "They're *exposing* their insides."

"And that's a good thing?" Deb asks. In our work, hard, fast, and exterior are the coins of the realm. Wild, primitive, and un-censored are the currency of our success. Exposed and personal are soapy, if not in outright bad taste.

"I'm not sure. They're not about heroic accomplishments or acrobatic feats. The language is so sensitive you have to quiet yourself down to listen to it. It's about the *inner* world."

"*Inner?*" Deb parrots me as if I'm speaking Japanese, but her eyes glitter with a dawning apprehension. We're on the brink of discovering a new genetic code. Should we proceed with this dangerous line of inquiry, or should we table it right now and return to the familiar safety of testosterone-fueled death-defying acts?

"I'll bring you some Sylvia Plath."

We're learning a new and forbidden language, the language of the interior. I inhale it more thirstily than I dare to admit; I've been longing for it for years.

"It's weird stuff." I toss back my Merlot.

And, just as any self-respecting guys would do, we close down the bar and stagger apelike into the night.

"Sometimes I think they're afraid of us," Deb says one night, lighting a cigarette.

"Why would they be?"

"We're like slaves that haven't yet realized there's such a thing as abolition."

"What would abolition look like? Quitting? I don't want to quit."

"I know."

We drink, thinking; we smoke for a while. "Maybe we should write our own material. For women."

"How?"

"I have no idea."

With self-effacing zeal, I ask John to write something "feminine" for us, a piece for three women. We invite a fellow actress to join us. All three of us win awards for our performances in *Disgrace*, in which three madwomen race around the stage giggling because they are in love with the same man. They wear old-fashioned dresses and straw bonnets and carry baskets filled with cheese. They leap and writhe and even kiss each other on the lips because they are sex-starved in their virginal white dresses. They just want to get laid, and while their lover screws around in far-off places, they attractively wait for him to rescue them from existential loneliness. Eventually, unsatisfied and unrequited, they toss themselves off a cliff.

So much for feminism.

Deb writes a play about Greek heroines called *Women in Ruins*. Medea is a sulky, misunderstood wife, Alcestis is a certifiable hypochondriac, and Phaedra is a drama queen with a drug problem. Hercules, Jason, and Creon are bumbling idiots, subject to the queens' neurotic whims.

We are getting closer.

I write a play about two women who can't tell themselves apart. Coming alive only in the embrace of "boys," the twin sisters inhabit a penumbral existence of blame and mistaken identity until one kills the other because the boys like her better.

Nice.

We barrel on like the blind leading the deaf to a concert by the mute. Everything we think and believe is coming unraveled. We are trying to find a new language, but the words elude us and the world isn't interested in our findings.

"A play about *what?*" the artistic director of the Intersection, an avant-garde theater venue, snorts.

"Two women."

"Why on earth would anyone be interested in a play about two women?" he asks.

This, I think, *is worse than I expected.*

"It's a poetic piece, lyrical, you know." I try to sound erudite; it seems to work for other people—

"Nobody wants to hear that shit."

—but it never works for me.

"It's about their interior life," I gabble. "It's like a dream. There's a rape," I add hopefully.

"A rape? Why didn't you say so? You can stage it in March."

I stage *TWIN* with all the bravado of a flock of geese flying north, honking and braying about my "new language." I'm going to carve a new sensibility for the theater, open the doors for the feminine muses of nuance and lyricism. It's going to be a theater of the interior where the threshold dissolves between outer and inner. I'm finding my voice.

Deb and I open the show to a full house. It's my breakout piece, my assertion of new values, my "women's play." I am speaking a truth that deeply matters to me. For the first time in my life, I feel authentic.

The critics yawn.

Reviewers who extolled my virtues as a dynamic member of the male ensemble, "athletic, crisp, and hilarious," remain unmoved by my precious interior piece. "Bloodless and stagnant," they call it. Where's the action? Where are the pyrotechnics?

I feel punched in the gut.

Something breaks inside me and my world caves in. I want to crawl out of my skin. I have exposed myself, once again, to a panel of critics who prefer the fireworks to the fire.

I want to hide under a rock.

The playground monitor creeps up behind me and hisses in my ear: *You're trying too hard.* I sit up straight and listen, praying for some relief. And then I understand. I've spent a lifetime straining to grasp a golden egg that will finally give me permission to be myself. There is no egg. There is no permission. I don't know how to find my inner permission, but it isn't in the hands of my father or my director or my fellow actors or the critics. It's time to grow up.

I quit the theater.

My life breaks into a hundred pieces and, though I don't yet know it, I am about to be reborn.

PART TWO

CHAPTER SIX

Door Number Three

WHAT ABOUT LOVE, YOU MIGHT WONDER? I HAD PLENTY of boyfriends. It was the 1970s. Pre-AIDS. Pre-epidemic-STD-levels. We were free, we were wild, we were on drugs. Experimentation was a way of life.

But love? I had no idea what that looked like. Like my mother, I thought it looked a lot like sex.

During my Hawkeye years, before I quit the theater, I waffled between two lovers. Jason was a beautiful New York Jew with a tendency toward melancholy. While I baked in the hot sun on a stunning black sand beach in Hawaii, Jason brooded under the nearest palm. He was fretting about his job.

"It doesn't have *meaning*," he mused, raising his voice to be heard over the guttering surf. Jason cashiered at a bookstore on Union Street that catered to expensively coiffed, surgically enhanced, sexually starved women. "But beautiful women flirt with me all day long. That's a perk."

"I'm not crazy about that particular perk," I said, rolling over to expose my back to the sun. "I wish you didn't have to flirt back quite so adeptly."

"It helps my self-esteem," he told me.

We bungled along, never saying what we meant and rarely meaning what we said. I had no idea what I wanted, and neither did the men I slammed into along the way. Jason moved to Vermont, and I hooked up with Bob.

A fellow Hawkeye, Bob brought out the wild, independent artist in me, while Jason (long-distance) elicited the tortured romantic. Bob and I contorted our athletic bodies onstage and in the bedroom as we toured our fiery shows up and down the state. Bob liberated a side of me that stayed up all night yelling about Brecht and Stanislavski in throes of spontaneous creative combustion. We danced and sang till dawn while he drummed maniacally on his ratty congas. With Jason, I pined (cross-country); with Bob, I erupted into creativity. It was a heady brew, and I juggled my two lovers for more than two years while I pondered, in an increasingly panicked state, *Jason or Bob? Bob or Jason?*

I thought that if I could just decide between Door Number One and Door Number Two, I would finally find myself. There I'd be, crouching behind the door, infuriated that it had taken me so long. "What the *hell* have you been waiting for?" I would ask, brushing off my jeans. "I've been huddled back here for years."

The problem? I thought I would find myself in a man's gaze. Some man, somewhere, would stamp my papers and provide the legitimacy I craved. On top of that, my biological clock was ticking so loudly, it thunked in my bloodstream like tennis shoes in the dryer. I was trying to choose between two impossible solutions to a problem that had nothing to do with either of them. *Who was I?* Was I a wife or an artist? Did I want children or an audience?

Have you ever given yourself a choice that couldn't be made? Have you chaired a meeting or gone to work while your brain ricocheted back and forth inside your skull like a squirrel on acid? Have you tortured yourself with *If that bus overtakes the red Camry, I'll choose Bob*, or *If the phone rings in the next three minutes, I'll choose Jason*? Have you consulted psychics, pulled tarot cards, thrown the I Ching until you wore a groove in your kitchen table with goddamn divination tools? I have.

Since my brain was snarled in a hopeless tangle of unanswerables, I started therapy. This was perhaps a good idea, given my ability to obfuscate, especially to myself.

"Pleeeease tell me," I pleaded to my hundred-dollars-an-hour sphinx in a blue pantsuit. "Which one am I supposed to choose?"

I'd been sowing wild oats for so long I was drowning in oatmeal. "Just *tell* me," I begged the silent therapist with the perfect haircut. But telling me was the one thing she could not do.

"I think," she said languorously, drawing out every hundred-dollar word, "that a third option is required."

"A *third* option," I wailed, imagining long lines of strange men straggling into my bedroom as I auditioned them for the part of Third Option. It was the last thing I wanted to hear. I was terrified that if I prolonged my dithering it would become a chronic condition. I did *not* want a third option.

I moped around, feeling lost and confused, unable to trust myself. I had no inner compass. *How do people choose anything?* I wondered. *How do they know what they want?* These were the right questions; I just kept coming up with the wrong answers.

Then I met David.

David Miller was a tall, handsome, blond auto mechanic. David was lanky, breezy, and a genius with his hands. He was neither fiery muse nor Byronic lover. He was far too sensible for all that. I didn't think sensible could be sexy, but my thinking was about to be overhauled along with my engine.

"You're going to need a new carburetor," he told me, wiping his hands on a shop rag. His eyes crinkled when he smiled. His voice was deep and resonant, and it made me want to curl up in his toolbox and take a nap.

Soon I was hanging around David's garage, watching him plunge his forearms into my engine compartment. His fingers danced among my valves. His hands glistened with my motor oil. I wanted David to apply those journeyman hands to my body. I wanted him to handle me as if I were a stubborn piston that refused to fire, tuning me to the perfect pitch of combustion. When I was around David, something bloomed in my chest that was unfamiliar and delicious. It was ease.

"Let's go to the Yuba River," I said to him. "I have to feed Susie's cat."

That weekend, we snaked up Interstate 80 to Nevada City on his motorcycle, and I confess to pressing myself so shamelessly against his back I could have asphyxiated a flea. I loved the way he handled the bike, slithering between oversized semis and melting around dangerous curves. David handled machinery like Rachmaninoff playing a piano concerto. Snuggling into his leather-jacketed back, I relaxed deep in my core.

We climbed off the bike, snapping me out of a sexual fantasy that involved coveralls and engine grease, and stripped down to our bathing suits. On the rocky trail down to the river, I stepped on a splinter the size of a carrot stick.

"Ouch!" I cried, trying not to look at the shaft of madrone that was sunk to the hilt into my heel.

David bent his long frame in two and took my foot in his hands. Gentle, calloused, motor-oil-stained hands. Then he returned to the bike, reached into a saddlebag, and pulled out the perfect tool. (David always has the perfect tool.) His touch was tender and proficient. "There you go," he said, sliding the splinter from my foot. I gazed into his eyes and combusted.

We climbed onto rocks that jutted from the swiftly moving river, and with blue water swirling at our feet, we talked about the future. "I'm at a turning point in my life," David told me. "I'm open for something new, though I'm not sure what it is."

It's me, I didn't say.

David owned a small bungalow and worked in the garage out back. After a lifetime of being around artists who lived from meal to meal in roach-infested squats, I found his stability profoundly calming. When I was around David, my nervous system dissolved; he was a spa treatment for my brain. I became aware that an essential part of me was softening, leaning into this person who was neither driven nor dissatisfied. He was never bored or critical. David was not ruled, as so many artists were, by neurotic ambition, and his tranquility was contagious.

"This," I inhaled sharply, "is love."

I had always heard that love, as portrayed by media mavens, was demonic, fetishistic, and homicidal. It caused people to shoot, maim, and betray one another, becoming scrawny, hopeless, or dead. No one ever taught me about ease. No one described the sensation, when your beloved sits on a rock in the middle of a river, of peace washing through your bones as if all your trials have suddenly ceased and the sun has come out on a winter's morning. No one explained the softening in the musculature of your being that feels like the melting of the polar ice cap. The breath released, the smile unfurling at the corner of your mouth, the light that fills his eyes when he watches you dance—these are the ingredients of love. Nobody dies or goes insane.

"I'm ready to have kids and settle down," David said, inspecting me with his droopy Midwestern eyes.

"Me too," I blurted.

All the women in my family had chosen men who tormented them, and I was determined to do it differently. The part of me that was exhausted from striving craved the ordinary moments of a well-lived life: children and carpools and burnt, hopeful Christmas cookies. "Me too," I repeated, and the sun cranked up into a glorious blaze, and for the first time in my life I did the absolutely right thing.

I married him.

CHAPTER SEVEN

My Thumb Works Just Fine

DAVID WAS THE DOOR NUMBER THREE OF MY DREAMS. I found prizes behind Door Number Three that I hadn't known existed: islands of calm, streams of serenity, and oceans of wellbeing. The peacefulness of his being eased my striving long enough for me to find a way home to myself. His steady love allowed me to drop into a deeper part of myself, the part that hid beneath cheap dreams of glory and fame. But that would come later.

First, there were problems to overcome. David didn't have any closet space.

When I moved into his bungalow, he said, "Put your stuff anywhere." But there wasn't a spare inch to be found because *his* stuff was crammed into every available crevice. We ate amid piles of invoices strewn with unmatched socks. I loved the guy, but frankly, he hoarded.

"We're going to have to find a bigger place," I informed him.

"What for?" he asked, prying his eyes off the football game.

"Because there's nowhere to put my stuff."

"Oh, don't worry about it. We'll clean out a closet for you."

Right.

"David?"

"What?" Did I detect a note of irritation climbing into his voice? Not David—he was the master of mellifluousness.

"What's that desiccated turd-like gob on the kitchen ceiling?"

"That's where I throw Larry's hamburger meat. He jumps for it," David added, smiling broadly. "It's cute."

Larry was David's cat. Larry hated me. He hissed like a malfunctioning gas valve the moment he met me and sprayed my cowboy boots so they stank every time I put them on. His feline intuition sensed an end to the happy-go-lucky bachelor days of hamburger dripping from ceilings and stacks of food-encrusted dishes in the sink where he joyfully snacked all day. He slunk around corners, eyeing me through slitted eyes, emitting reptilelike warnings that he would outwit me in this struggle to the death for David's affections.

"I'm going to wash it off," I announced, doing that thing women do when they move in with their boyfriends—namely, clean their houses. Back went the hair into a ponytail, on slid the gloves, out poured the bleach, up piled the sponges and scrapers I had assembled for the job. But the rock-solid year-old hamburger was glued to the ceiling like epoxy; not even a chisel could take it off.

"David?" I called, my voice quivering.

"Now what is it?" He was re-evaluating his mental stability for inviting someone like me to come and live with him.

"It doesn't come off the ceiling."

"So leave it *on* the ceiling."

Oh ... my ... God. He couldn't possibly think it was okay to leave ancient, desiccated, rotten, calcified hamburger meat on the kitchen ceiling. *Could he?*

David was not raised by my mother, the Etiquette Czar. That is, David didn't care what knife he used or which fork came first, or even whether globs of ancient animal flesh adhered permanently to his ceilings. When it came to table manners, he preferred to use his fingers, thank you very much. I found this endearing, especially when we had dinner with the Etiquette Czar herself.

"He's got nice legs, I'll give him that," she relented. I considered myself lucky she didn't want to give him a trial run, like she had with my older sister's (then-seventeen-year-old) boyfriend. Mama eyed David's technique of shoveling peas onto his fork with the spatulate part of his thumb.

I waited.

"Here, David," she said after a freighted pause, handing him a heel of bread. "Use this to push the peas if you absolutely refuse to use a knife."

"No thanks, Mrs. Teague," David said, masticating vigorously. "My thumb works just fine."

Boom! I chortled like a fat man in a pastry shop. *No thanks, Mrs. Teague*, I cackled inside my brain. *My thumb works just fine!*

David was The One for me.

Here's what I knew about marriage:

My father "didn't have the hammer to drive the nail," according to my mother, and we all know how important the hammer was to her. (Or was it the nail?) My stepfather was a depressive gay man who used alcohol to blunt his agony because he was living someone else's life. My mother did me the favor of imparting to me her big gobsmacking secret, which was that men's dicks were their only asset, and between my parents and sisters, eleven out of fourteen sacred matrimonial contracts had collapsed into bitter, home-wrecking divorces by the time I finally found the nerve to say "I do." I considered the alternatives: "Maybe I do"? "Hopefully I will"? Or how about "I'll try"?

David informed me that if I ever cheated on him, he would take our prospectively darling children and leave me behind in a cloud of exhaust. (He's good with automotive metaphors.) I was impressed. Here was a man who meant what he said. "I would never," I swore. I considered that my parents had cheated on each other and wondered if I had the fidelity gene required to back up this promise.

I can do this, I told myself, quaking ever so slightly in my grown-up shoes.

People talk about all the bells and whistles of falling in love, all the thunder and lightning and earth-shaking and volcanic eruptions, until it feels like it should be a Jules Verne novel or *War of the Worlds*. But I think, and I know I'm right about this, that falling in love is more about the day-to-day stuff. Are you happy to stain-stick his motor oil–stained T-shirt? Do you love the way he drives a car? Do you smile at the collection of wind-up toys in his bedside drawer? If all these things are true . . .

Marry him.

We traded David's house for a bigger model in which I could actually unpack, and we got married. My mother didn't come to the wedding because she had a policy about coming to her children's weddings: she didn't. All my theater friends and ex-boyfriends were there, and all of David's lanky blonde ex-girl-friends were there, too. The wedding photos looked like a re-union of Sex and Love Addicts Anonymous. But it was the eighties, and we all got along famously even if we did snort drugs in the bathroom with the catering staff and throw up at the reception because the boat ride was so rocky.

Before the nauseating boat ride, we were married in slap-dash fashion in our backyard with taped music and stoned guests and children underfoot and me in hippie headgear and six-inch stilettos—in the mud, because it was drizzling. My dad gave me away. I'm not sure he ever possessed me enough to give me away in the first place, but at least he showed up, unlike other parents I could mention but won't. He gave me away, flirted with all my friends, and then left, in that order. The joy of this rare appearance made me feel—as it always did—special.

Forty years later, we still have a piece of wedding cake in our freezer. Our friends look at us as if we're mad, but we think it's romantic. Or maybe we're afraid that if we throw it away, the spell will be broken.

Everybody needs something to believe in.

CHAPTER EIGHT

I Love You So Much I'm Exploding

I WANTED TO HAVE KIDS, BUT SINCE I WAS STILL WORKING in the theater when I married David, I was afraid they would inhibit my rise to stardom. Would I miss a career-defining performance? Could I walk on my hands with a baby in my belly?

But David's tireless goodwill, not to mention his indefatigable sperm, overcame my qualms. Two years after we married, at the age of thirty-three, I discovered that I was pregnant with Kyle, and something moved deep inside me. It was a volcanic kind of joy. My bulky, dark ambition had to move over to make room for this tiny being that needed all of my blood and bones and sinew to grow his arms and legs and little toes. I couldn't be Somebody and be a Mom at the same time. Somebody was dragged off-stage, kicking and screaming, and Mom, blinking and confused, was left behind.

Kyle appeared like the sun breaking through a rain cloud, one tiny fist proclaiming his magnificence. His little being induced spasms of adoration in everyone who laid eyes on him—

well, in David and me. (Not everyone is capable of rapture.)

"I want Cheetos for lunch!" Kyle, two years old, pounded the table with a fist.

"Absolutely not," I replied. "Eat your spinach."

"Cheetos?" Tears glistened in his wide, helpless eyes.

I passed the Cheetos. (I could not say no.)

He read every copy of his *Ranger Rick* magazines from cover to cover, informing us about the mating habits of platypuses and the left-handedness of polar bears. (Kyle: "Did you know that honeybees have hairs on their eyeballs?" Me: "I did not.") He tackled science experiments with the passion of a poet.

And me? I raced around burning cookies and showing up late for rehearsal. I was a demented cocktail of *Leave It to Beaver* and Codependents Anonymous, effortlessly blending the frenetic race to accomplish something with the biological urge to nurse something, resulting in a glassy-eyed mom-bot who believed children should be smothered with love. I really didn't have a clue how this was done. My own mother had:

1. Left half her children behind in an ugly divorce
2. Hired nannies to handle the other half
3. Popped us into boarding school when times got tough
4. Changed the locks

Kyle came out wailing and fighting and insisting on his rights, challenging every authority he encountered. I watched him struggle and suffer and try to find his way, and his heartbreak became my heartbreak. You cannot change a child's course; all you can do is provide snacks.

CYNTHIA MOORE

When he was born, David and I thought Kyle was the smartest child ever created. We carted him around and made him perform for our friends. Now, when people parade their children around in this (*oh-so-tasteless*) way, I try not to judge them. We were drunk on love.

Poor Kyle. He carried all the weight of our parental pride as if he were a brand-new marketing product we had designed and manufactured ourselves. How would he find a way to be who he was?

He was a too-bright kid with a million interests and the attention span of a gnat. Like most boys, he suffered agonies behind his school desk, itching to race outside and tear things apart. He wanted to build things and deconstruct things and understand how they worked, not read about them in books. Kyle would bang into the world until he figured it out. But he would, thanks to his unquenchable curiosity, figure it out. He would navigate his teen years like a ballistic missile, throwing himself headlong into every risk, until he could survive the ill-designed system with unimpeachable integrity.

"Why should I respect authorities just because they tell me to?" he questioned. Secretly, I was proud of his refusal to collude with idiots.

Five years later, Eliza came along, our golden-haired cherub. She stormed onto the scene, demanding respect even though she was only nineteen inches tall. Her emotions filled the house, sweeping through rooms with all the fury of a tornado. Luckily for her, our hubris was exhausted, so we didn't parade her around the neighborhood or send out a newsletter every time she burped. We just let her be our "darling girl," sunny and con-

84

fident as the potentate of a small country, freshly arrived to transform us all.

Eliza was fearless and adventurous; when David threw her into the air, she laughed like a little monkey. She fell off play structures and climbed back up to the top. An artist from the start, she drew endless pictures of suns wearing sunglasses, beaming down on a happy family of four. Hanging upside down in her chair at the dinner table, she made us all laugh. "I'm talking to my planet," she'd announce, her little legs waving in the air.

When I came into her room one morning, she informed me, "My dream people told me not to wake up."

"Who are your dream people?"

"They live inside the mattress."

Eliza snuggled into the curvature of my body, warm as fresh-baked bread. If Kyle was a force of nature, rappelling off me to catapult through space, Eliza was a puppy in my lap.

When these two came along, I was shipwrecked. As a person who was still figuring out what love was, I floundered, unable to stay afloat in these wild emotional currents. No one survives children intact.

My children, by the way, look like teeny-tiny versions of David. Blond, lanky, and unperturbed. *Wait.* Wasn't I the one who did all the hard work to eject them into the world? Couldn't I at least have gotten a nose? An eyebrow? But no. Tiny blond Davids, right down to their toenails, as if I have no gene pool at all.

As I observe their progress, gnawing my fingernails in paroxysms of lovesick worry, I try to keep my mouth shut and my useless maternal perseverations to myself. Sometimes my lips are clamped so tightly together it sounds like *mmphgrpplbmkknt.*

My kids understand.

It means, "I love you so much I'm exploding."

When I quit the theater, Eliza was a baby. Kyle was six. I was standing at a precipice without an identity. Who the hell was I? I had failed as an artist.

"I'll give myself nine months," I told my friend Deb (who had returned to Vermont) over the phone. "At the end of nine months I'll give birth to a new version of myself."

Like a pregnancy, I thought the dismemberment of my personality would be a finite event. "Maybe I'll become a nurse," I added, imagining a life of solicitous bandage-changing and a crisp, white identity. Anything but bodies hurled against walls amid comrades peering furtively at my breasts.

I felt sick. Not having a fabricated self was worse than having no self at all. I still taught theater to sixth-graders, but that wasn't an identity.

"I'm going to be a—a—" I paused, grabbing the Yellow Pages and jabbing my finger at the first profession I saw. "A steel processor—or, no, here's a good one—staplers, nailers, and tackers. I'm going to be a stapler, nailer, and tacker," I informed Deb in a funereal tone. "I could be good at that."

She didn't deign to answer me, so I decided to go back to school and become a shrink. Shrinks, unlike artists, have a guaranteed niche in the world. Shrinks inhabit that murky interior place that I craved, nosing like a heat-seeking missile toward the truth.

"What do you think about shrinks?" I asked Deb.

Once again, she didn't deign to answer, but I took that as a good sign and hightailed it to the nearest graduate school before she could tell me what she really thought.

Deb directed Shakespeare in a barn in central Vermont, and her cast was culled from butchers and farmers and unemployed milkmen. There was always a last-minute problem.

"I give up," she told me during one of our Tuesday-morning phone seminars. Shifting the phone to my other ear, I slurped my old lady coffee substitute, which sorely lacked the psychotic buzz of the real deal. I burned my tongue and yelped with pain.

"What's wrong?" I asked, when I'd recovered enough to speak. I had already enrolled in shrink school and was hopefully on the way to a new and better me.

"My Prospero has an Elks Club meeting and Ariel has the mumps," she moaned.

"How long till you open?" I asked.

"Two weeks," she said.

"Every show you've ever done, you've wanted to quit two weeks before it opened." (You can see that the study of psychology was already having a salutary effect on me. I was analyzing everyone I met.) "Get over the hump."

"I guess you're right," she muttered, though she wasn't happy about it.

"I'm writing a novel," I admitted, twirling the phone cord around my finger (this was back when phones were attached to walls). "I can't seem to stop myself. It's like having a tapeworm."

"That's good! What's it about?"

"I don't know."

"Good, Cynthia. You're not supposed to know what it's about. You're supposed to relax and trust the process."

"Oh, great." Now I was the one who wasn't happy.

"Listen," she said. "Send me the chapters you've written."

I held my breath. "But—"

"Send me the chapters you've written and shut up. I don't want to hear another word out of your mouth."

"Okay," I said in a four-year-old voice.

"We have to keep going," Deb told me. "That's what artists do. They go on trying to find the thread, even though the thread keeps getting lost. We're here to remind each other of our purpose."

"I guess," I murmured. My purpose seemed a million miles away.

"When we're eighty years old," said Deb, "we'll look back on these conversations and realize that they were a trail of breadcrumbs leading us back to the path. Like Rilke's *Letters to a Young Poet*. To begin with, we've documented every possible form of resistance known to artists."

"The world isn't ready for my art."

"I can't do this without national funding."

"I can't do this in a male-dominated culture."

"I can't do this without Xanax."

By now we were laughing.

"I can't do this with my husband in the house."

"I can't do this without a gallon of espresso—"

"—brought to my desk—"

"—by my personal assistant—"

"—who looks like Brad Pitt."

"Let's face it," Deb said, pausing for breath. "There are so many reasons we can't do this, we'd better just keep on doing it. What do you say?"

"You're so right."

"Bye, Cynthia."

"Bye, Deb."

"Talk to you next week."

Click.

CHAPTER NINE

On Becoming
an Embarrassment

"I DON'T SEE WHY MY PARENTS GETTING DIVORCED WHEN I was one year old should have a negative effect on my career," I whine.

Silence from Dr. Tibble, the latest in the sequence of mental health personnel I have been required to hire since I quit the theater and enrolled in a master's program. To get a master's degree, it seems I have to be in therapy, presumably to prevent me from unleashing my history on unsuspecting clients. I need more therapy like a fish needs a phone.

"I mean, I'm fine. I'm so over all that. Who *cares*?"

More silence. (The more you pay, it seems, the less they respond.)

"Okay, so I'm glad we had this talk. How much do I owe you?"

"Cynthia, how do you *feel* about your parents' divorce?" (The sphinx speaks.)

"Jeez, how do I know?"

After spending $2,500, I feel sad; $5,000 after that, I feel devastated, and with $10,000 in the hole, I am a sloppy mess of hypersensitive volatility. But Dr. Tibble is just doing her job, which is to give me a safe place to fall apart. In order to dismantle my overdrive, I have to stop running. I have to step into the fire that is my emotional truth, even if it burns me to a crisp.

I have to start feeling.

"I feel fine about the divorce," I lie.

But Dr. Tibble doesn't bite. "Let's try that again," she says, gently, until the dam finally breaks. She has the patience of a tortoise and the will of a steam engine. I fall, if expensively, apart.

I have to sort through the moments when I learned to run away from pain. Each one requires me to make a fresh commitment. Can I feel the loss of my father when my mother dragged me to Nassau? Can I face the day we left my little sister in an institution, driving away from her anguished six-year-old face? Can I feel the collapse in my chest when I understood, at eleven, that I would never go home again? Each memory unravels the soft web of my pretenses. I have been hard as ice, and none of it is real. Can I bare my honest self?

"This is a very young part of me that I locked away," I tell Dr. Tibble.

"That's right."

I have to find the missing pieces. I have to comb through my life and claim my place in it. I have to weed through the longing for masculine approval and connect with my real, unwanted self, which is as raw and vulnerable as an ugly little duckling.

"I can't go outside like this," I cry. "I feel naked."

"You *are* naked," she says simply.

"You mean, let people see me like this? They'll be horrified."

"It doesn't matter what people think. Your job is to take care of your tender heart and be fully who you are," she says.

Imagine that, I think.

That's when I catch fire. I want to help other people navigate this soft-tissue place. I want to help them deconstruct themselves. I want to come up with creative ways to put Humpty Dumpty together again. I feel truly alive for the first time in my adult life, and this gives me a vision: I will develop a program for accelerated psychological restructuring.

I hunker into my graduate program, determined to manufacture my very own Frankenstein model of therapeutic reconstruction. I will not just nod and shudder empathically like analysts do—I will help people build quick and effective new selves. I will speed up this process!

I devour Freud and Jung and Adler and Sullivan and salivate my way through endless texts of symptomatology and psychopathologies, collecting diagnoses like rare stamps. I have found my purpose.

"You're a narcissist," I tell my friend Charles over coffee at Peet's. "It explains why you want every conversation to be about you. Luckily," I add, "I'm codependent, so every conversation can *be* about you." I smile widely, slurping my decaf, and wonder why Charles looks sour.

"We're histrionics," I tell Deb over the phone. "That's why we were in the theater. We are overly dramatic," I add in a whisper, as if she has never suspected this. I feel as proud as someone who's unearthed a rare lexicon of brand-new astrological signs.

"You have obsessive-compulsive disorder," I announce to David one night over dinner. "That's why you line up your tools in those perfect little rows." David, inured to these outbursts, helps himself to the Parmesan.

Friends and family ignore me. I have become an embarrassment, spouting diagnoses on a daily basis. "Pablo," I wail at my friend Joan, "is a sociopath. *Don't* let him house-sit your cat."

Having decided that I'm a recovering narcissistic histrionic codependent with post-traumatic stress disorder, I feel renewed.

"Mom! What's for dinner?"

"Ask Dad. Mom's going to school tonight." Why do moms refer to themselves in the third person? Because we are tiny, flawed humans scrambling to fill the shoes of a gigantic all-powerful Mom-goddess in the sky.

"Weird to go to school at *night*."

"You said it."

I ingest the entire DSM-IV while filling Kyle's and Eliza's lunch boxes, and it probably scars them for life. The DSM (the Holy Bible of psychopathology) is a morbid compilation of dead-end diagnoses. It's a paradigm of hopelessness born from an inferiority complex that forced its compilers to devise impressive lists of diseases in an impersonation of science, though we all know that the genius of Freud and Jung and Whitaker lay in their intuitive artistry. But scientists have lorded it over artists in the credibility department for the past two hundred years (Bacon, I think, is to blame for this); therefore artistry must be codified into lists. And the lists are compiled of chronic and acute malfunctions, just like religious inventories of sins. The DSM's catalog of depressing diagnoses is making me diagnostically depressed.

Luckily, I discover Jung. Jung was one of the few forefathers of modern psychology who saw a transcendent capacity in the human psyche. Jung believed that we suffer in order to grow. We break to become whole. We individuate from our cultural/parental constructs in order to connect with a Self that is numinous and purposive. In the first half of life, we respond to external expectations and pressures, and in the second half, we find the courage to be who we are. This sets off fireworks in my brain.

Jung tows me through the symptoms, diagnostic codes, and pathological thickets of schizophreniform disorder, trichotillomania with trichophagia, and derealization syndrome. I gobble up his work on dreams, archetypes, and the Great Feminine while churning out reports on agoraphobia. A new awareness is kindling in me, and I burn to bring it into practice.

CHAPTER TEN

A Fully Realized Hotbed of Compulsive Ideas

JUST BECAUSE MY PSYCHOPATHOLOGY PROFESSOR INSISTS ON referring to the plural of diagnosis *as* diagnosises *does* not *mean he's a moron.* I grit my teeth and try not to look like a Grammar Nazi. Because the truth is, like my mother, I am a despot when it comes to the English language. Smoke belches from my eye sockets.

My mother, in addition to being the Etiquette Czar, was the original Grammar Nazi. "*Never* say," she once gasped, clutching her chest, "that you are going to *lay* down!" *Snort, heave*—"It's *lie*! And darling, *irregardless*"—she rolled her eyes as if about to expire—"is *not* a word."

"The dual diagnosises are the most difficult," drones the psychopathology professor with the bulbous nose, causing me to jerk violently in my chair. In actuality, he is an excellent diagnostician who works for an impressive hospital, and he is even a good teacher. He's just, like most Americans, a full-fledged moron when it comes to grammar. Grinding my teeth, I forge through six months of Psychopathology I and II, by the end of which time I am known as "that difficult older student" who insists on writing her final paper about Jung's flaphappy view of symptomatology. (Jung wrote that our neurotic symptoms are our personal map to freedom. *Ta-da!*)

"We don't study *Jung* in this program," Professor Grammar Moron says, as if I have quoted Mickey Mouse.

"Maybe you ought to," I snap. I am forty years old, and I don't ingest patriarchal theories without an attitude. Perhaps I am still fighting male authority, but it's clear to me that Jung was the only evolved thinker in the bunch. I am willing to read dead white guys until I can no longer see the page, but I will damn well form my own conclusions.

Our neuroses, according to Jung, guide us toward not only personal growth but cultural healing as well. Rather than being incurable signs of illness, they are trail markers to wellness. The more conscious we become, the more we repair our broken society. *Reconstructive psychotherapy*, I think with a thrill. I am salivating.

"You're *doing* too much, Cynthia," Susan drawls in a bored voice, flipping through the transcript of my first client session. I am a therapist-in-training at a low-fee clinic, and Susan is my supervisor—an angular woman in a shapeless dress.

When I started training, I almost had a panic attack when my first client walked into the room. *She can see that I'm a total fraud,* my brain squeaked inside my frozen face. "And so," I bleated like a pig in heat, "what brings you here today?'

"I'm having trouble in my marriage," she said, wiping her eyes.

"Tell me what's happening," I murmured in a soothing tone, holding my chin in one hand and crossing my legs so I would at least look like a therapist. I wondered, *Does this look awkward?* I moved the chin to the other hand and re-crossed my legs. *Whatever you do, don't look at the clock*, I reminded myself.

She seemed assuaged by my professional posturing because she continued as though there were no impostors in the room masquerading as therapists. "I think he might be having an affair."

"An affair?" I sympathetically drawled, thinking, *What an asshole!* "What makes you think that?"

She started to sob and, panicking, I threw a box of Kleenex at her. "Maybe you should leave him," I suggested in a helpful tone.

She stopped crying and looked at me in astonishment. "Leave him?" she echoed. "We've been married for twenty-three years."

I nodded understandingly. "So don't leave him."

She looked bewildered. "*Don't* leave him?"

"Listen," I said, willing myself to stay calm, telling myself that a marriage could not be destroyed in one fifty-minute session. "Let's start over. How do you *feel*?"

The woman emitted a gusty sigh of relief. "I'm *so* hurt!"

"Tell me how hurt you are," I prodded, my shoulders realizing that they no longer needed to stuff themselves into my ears.

And she did. She told me how confused she was and how angry she felt until, mercifully, the fifty minutes elapsed and I, mopping my brow, showed her to the door.

"Can I come back next week?" she pleaded.

An embarrassing wave of triumph washed over me. Fixing a somber expression on my face, I flipped open my notebook. "I'll check my schedule," I said, even though it was as blank as a nun's dance card.

"I happen to have a one o'clock next Tuesday," I said. "Will that work?"

Two weeks later, while reviewing the transcript, my supervisor sighs. She flips through my notes with blunt, unpainted fingers. "You need to relax, Cynthia. It's not your job to fix these people."

"But," I say, "I have so many ideas on how to help them!"

Susan raises her head and glares at me over her half-moon reading glasses. Her eyes are as cold as arctic char.

"Well, keep them," she intones, "to yourself."

"I want another supervisor," I say during my second year at the Counseling Center. Susan is in the past—I'm now being supervised by Matthew. "After working with my women's group, three of them are off their antidepressants and the other two are feeling better than they have in years."

"That's a dangerous claim," asserts Matthew. "What makes you think it has anything to do with your group?"

"They tell me it's because of the group. Because of the guided meditations I've been leading."

"Guided meditations?"

I'm used to the raised eyebrow and the thinly disguised urge to regurgitate, but I fight for my innovative rights, fully aware that therapists, like children of a certain era, are supposed to be seen and not heard. My various supervisors have been trying to train me to "do less" for over a year. Doing less, for better or worse, is not my style.

"I want another supervisor," I storm. "Someone who will let me try out new techniques."

"Psychotherapy is not about *techniques*, Cynthia."

"I know you think that. That's why I'm asking you to step aside."

"Well, I won't." Matthew—a rugged, bearded man who likes to play by the rules, walk the line, and not rock the boat—thinks (and he's correct) that I am trouble. "We don't experiment on clients as if they are guinea pigs," he finishes.

"I do," I retort. I have evolved from my clumsy attempts to give clients advice. Now I am experimenting with guiding them toward their own inner advice-dispensers, their own playground monitors, so to speak. "I try new things every week, and these women are more hopeful than they've been in ages. One of them is ready to leave her husband."

"And that's a good thing?"

"He's been abusing her for nine years."

"I see." Matthew chews on his beard, which grows long and bedraggled around the edges of his mouth. I see a flicker of vulnerability in his eyes, and suddenly I know that he doesn't want me to replace him. "Let's do this," he says at last. "I'll continue supervising you for three weeks. You can try your new techniques and we'll talk about their efficacy. If, at the end of three weeks, you still feel I'm not the best person to support you, I'll step aside and you can work with Helen Burk instead."

"Deal," I say.

After three weeks, Matthew settles himself on the polyester couch and turns an anticipatory eye on me. I always have a breakthrough to report, and my clients are transforming so rapidly that it's like watching Dr. Phil on fast-forward. I'm using a combination of improvisation and visualization techniques to blast through resistance and get people in touch with their inner playground monitors. My accelerated therapy techniques are working.

I describe my Tuesday-night women's group to Matthew.

"Drop inside," I intoned to the six women present, "and move through the layers of anger and hurt until you reach the center of yourself. There, you'll find a still and quiet place."

The women settled in their seats, their nervous laughter silenced as they focused inward. I was in my element.

"That quiet place is your True Self, whole and undamaged," I said.

I loved this work. It never failed to move me. My own hidden self had been locked away for so long. I was thrilled to help others find theirs.

Tears formed in Anna's eyes. Lorraine took deep, relaxing breaths. *We all need guidance*, I thought, *and it's inside us.*

"Emanating from that stillness, you'll hear a message. Listen carefully. Reject nothing."

Six women scrunched up their faces as if they were trying to pick up radio signals from Mars. I checked my watch and popped a breath mint. The clock on the wall ticked on.

After a few minutes, I asked them to open their eyes. Gabbling excitedly, they all spoke at once. "I'm supposed to write a book," cried Jackie, looking stunned.

"Take my power back!" Lorraine pumped her fist.

Janet, the woman who had been abused by her husband for nine years, inhaled softly and said, "It's time to walk away from Jim."

I choked on my breath mint and stared at Janet. She had been fighting this decision for years. Everyone cheered, and—I admit it—the word *breakthrough* blinked on and off in my brain like a neon sign. I relaxed in the warm sense of accomplishment as the women chattered about the messages they'd received. I needed these breakthroughs like I needed air. They made me feel worthwhile.

When I finish describing the session, I ask Matthew in a small voice, "Am I responsible for their breakthroughs?" I pause. "Or would they be happening without me?"

"You're doing good work with these women, Cynthia," Matthew admits. "You should take pride in your success."

It's as if my daddy has parted the clouds and beamed the light of God right down on my unworthy head. It's the approval I've been waiting for my whole life. I stare at Matthew, blinking like a baby owl. He sees the wounded part of me that needs affirmation, and he gives it to me. It's strong medicine. I absorb his words into my bloodstream, and they give me the courage to go on.

"I'm hot for my supervisor," I tell my sister Jill.

"Isn't that normal?" she asks. "Don't all interns have—what do they call it?—erotic transference to their supervisors? Like teachers and priests?"

"I want to throw him on the couch and rip off his Tevas when he tells me I'm doing a good job. But I can't ruin my marriage," I wail, thinking of ten years of wedded bliss—not to mention David's assurance that he will disappear with the children into a cloud of exhaust if I cheat on him.

"Don't *sleep* with him," Jill counsels. "Just enjoy feeling hot for him."

What a concept, I think. To lust without consummation has never occurred to me.

I squirm in my chair through the next few months of Matthew's supervision, alternately adoring him as we fling aside the rules of psychotherapy and feeling like a beloved child when he supports my treatment choices. By the end of my internship, I am still monogamous and a fully realized hotbed of compulsive ideas. (It will be years before I stop trying to remodel my clients.)

My job, I think, is to give them the tools to change. I want to reach into the basement of their psyches and tweak their furnaces so they will stop belching foul smoke every time their mothers come to dinner. I want to repair the highway between their brains and their nervous systems so the tractor-trailers of their emotions will not fly off the overpass. I want to rebuild their engines and overhaul their transmissions.

I am doing too much.

CHAPTER ELEVEN

God Knows, She Tried

IN ADDITION TO REMODELING MY CLIENTS, I SEEK TO improve myself every minute of every day. I have a built-in mechanism that rejects what is actually happening in favor of a more idealized version. This leads to a flurry of vicious upgrading. Steam shoots from my ears, and my teeth ache from the pressure of a thousand pounds of effort rumbling through my nervous system twenty-four seven. *Try harder.* Here's what my internal command center sounds like:

> *Lose weight*
> *Be happy*
> *End homelessness*
> *Get enlightened*
> *Avoid documentaries about Somalia, which will only depress you*
> *Do chin exercises*

I am about to explode from so much effort, rupturing my skin bag and spraying rib fragments all over my clean kitchen floor. My eulogy will read, *Here lies Cynthia Moore. God knows, she tried.*

Halfway through my internship at the Counseling Center, as I am clocking hundreds of client hours in bleak, fluorescent-lit rooms, my adrenals crash. I can't get out of bed without a strong caffe latte, can't get through the morning without a double espresso, can't get to dinnertime without a midafternoon dose of high-octane caffeine. By bedtime, I'm a beached whale of comatose fatigue.

You may be smart enough to piece together the fact that I am single-handedly trying to rescue everyone in the Western Hemisphere with the coincidence that my nervous system is going on strike. *I can't*, my body informs me, *pull this off.*

My response? More caffeine.

"Cynthia," whines a sixty-year-old shut-in who has no money and is afraid to leave her house. "It's too hard for me to get across town. Could you come to my house and play gin rummy with me?"

I drive to her home, park my car, go inside, and play gin rummy with her every Wednesday for two years. She always beats me. Is there any therapy in it? Well, she feels better when she wins.

"Tom just pulled a knife on me," weeps Crystal over the phone at 1:00 a.m., waking me from a tortured sleep. "But I can't leave him because I still love him. I believe he can change." Crystal has four kids under the age of eight.

"You have to leave him *now*, Crystal, or someone will get hurt."

After twenty minutes of being cajoled on the phone, Crystal finally agrees.

"I'll contact the women's shelter," I say. "They'll pick you up in an unmarked van."

Four phone calls later, the van drives Crystal and her four kids, their teddy bears, and their black eyes to a secret location in Martinez. I hang up the phone at 2:00 a.m., heave a sigh of relief, and go back to bed.

A few days later, another client begs, "I really need this job and you're the only one who knows me, Cynthia. Can you write me a reference that doesn't, like, mention my borderline personality disorder?"

"Of course I can, Kay."

I drag myself home and climb under the covers.

"*Mom!*"

(I try ignoring my children, hoping they will go away.)

"I *need* you."

(Ignoring them never works.)

"I'm trying to get some sleep, honey. I'm so exhausted."

"But I *need* you. Kyle says I can't have his bug box."

I drag myself from my bed, my tank so bone-dry I am running on fumes and wishes, and confront Kyle, who sits calmly in the kitchen constructing a bridge out of toothpicks. "What the hell is a bug box?" I ask him.

"It's something I made," he answers complacently. "She wants it and she can't have it."

Eliza cranks up the amplifier on her vocal cords until her howls rattle the frying pans.

"David!" I scream.

Enter David, calm and serene. David locates the aforesaid bug box (a toilet paper roll with screened ends), makes a second one for Eliza, and fries up a couple of grilled cheese sandwiches, dispersing the tension and allowing me to climb back into bed.

The next day, I go to the doctor and explain my symptom: all I want to do is sleep.

"Oh my God." He visibly pales.

"What is it?"

"Your adrenals have flatlined. I've never seen anything like it."

Well, that explains the fatigue.

"You've got to stop trying to save the world, Cynthia. You're wearing yourself out," he says. *Can you give me a pill for that?*

I'm no longer striving to be Someone. Instead, I'm trying to save Everyone. *Somebody stop me.*

He scribbles a prescription for frozen pig adrenaline to be injected into my butt. Ice-cold ass notwithstanding, I feel better within a month. My caffeine intake diminishes, and I complete my internship, grab a master's degree, and crank right back up to where I was before: rescuing my clients, psychoanalyzing my friends, and parenting my young children at ninety miles per hour. I am the dancer in the red shoes, compelled to keep dancing, unable to stop even after falling off the brink of exhaustion.

I want to be like the Buddhists I know who glide around taking deep breaths and wearing catlike smiles that say, *I'm so above whatever you're obsessing about right now.*

I long to retreat to a remote, cloudy nest high above the murky bogs of suffering. Aching for relief from myself, I take up meditation. Most people, I wager, take up meditation for that reason—i.e., get me out of here!

I exploit meditation for that transcendental state that promises respite from the turmoil. (An experienced Buddhist would call this *aversion*.) It will be years before I realize that turmoil is what I need to face. Buddhist practice is about staying present with whatever is there, not running like hell in the opposite direction.

But for now, my plan is to *om* my way into blissful avoidance. *Don't worry*, I whisper between clenched teeth. *Be happy.*

"Mom?"

"Don't bother Mom. She's meditating."

"She's been meditating for *hours*." (Translation: five minutes.)

I unfold my cramped legs, plaster a beatific smile on my face, and step out of the Volkswagen van. We are camping, and I have spent three weeks enclosed in a tiny metal box with two noisy children and one spiritually indifferent husband. I am meditating in order to keep a tight lid on the bitch fest that will, at any moment, erupt from between my clamped, meditating teeth.

"*Mom!*"

"*What?*"

"I need you!"

"You *have* me."

"No, I *need* you to come and look at what Kyle did to my ant hotel!"

I step down from the van—*remember the bliss; we are all One*—and trip over a plastic truck.

"*Fuck*," I say. Kyle's battalion of vehicles is arrayed in perfect, symmetrical lines (obsessive-compulsive disorder?) right where my foot lands when I emerge from the van.

"I thought," observes David wryly, "you were getting blissed out."

"I *am* blissed out, goddammit. That's why I'm so fucking *cranky* right now."

"Mommy gets mad when she meditates," Eliza whispers to her father.

"*I do not.*"

The little smiles twitching around the corners of their lips do nothing to lighten my mood, and I stomp off to find the famous ant hotel. "Show me, Eliza. What did he do?"

Tears course down her four-year-old cheeks. "He broke it!"

The ant hotel is a clump of mud and sticks, and two sticks have been neatly broken in half. This was unnecessary, it seems to me, in light of the fact that we are all One. "*Kyle!*"

My nine-year-old son rambles out of the bush where he has been constructing an ingenious badger house with bungee cords and rope. "What?" he says.

"Eliza says you broke her hotel, and I'm wondering"—note the therapeutic turn of phrase—"why you would do such a thing."

"Because she's an annoying little toad."

"*Kyle.*"

"You asked me why, Mom, and I told you." Kyle turns to go, satisfied with the eloquence of his reasoning.

"You're supposed to *love* your little sister, for Christ's sake. We are all One here, Kyle—don't you *get* it?"

Kyle starts to cry, whereupon Eliza, seeing a chance to outshine him in the one area over which she has absolute domain, wails louder.

"Will you kids shut the hell up and let a person think for a minute?" I take a deep breath, panicking. *What happened to my bliss? Where's my sanctuary of inner peace?* "Jeez! It's like a nuthouse around here."

This, of course, is David's cue to swoop in and rescue us all from our own psychoses. He strolls up, clear-eyed and brown from the sun, smiling faintly at the feast of histrionics we have once again, like manic chefs, whipped up for ourselves. "Who wants to go kayaking?" he asks.

The children cheer up and traipse happily after their dad while I stand amid the towering redwood trees watching my family waddle away from me, wondering how a person is supposed to know the first goddamn thing about parenting.

I could probably blame my parents' alcoholism, divorce, and general cluelessness, but I'm fed up to my nostrils with therapy, so I pop open a bag of chips and head for the picnic table to stuff my face.

I have been in graduate school for six years (don't laugh—it takes me eight to get my master's) when we find our cabin on a lake. David goes off to reconstruct our fixer-upper with all his obsessive-compulsive verve.

"David!" I scream into the telephone, knee-deep in dirty laundry, my back pressed against the laundry room door as the kids' bickering in the other room rises to a crisis of international proportions and my unfinished homework steams on my desk.

"What is it, honey?"

"I CAN'T DO THIS." *This*, of course, is what millions of women all across America are doing: raising two (or more) beautiful (or not) children who have everything they need (or don't). I can't think about the mothers in the "don't" category, immigrant moms with six children who are in terror of being deported. I can't even manage two well-adjusted middle-class kids in private schools with college funds fattening in the bank.

"I don't know how to be a mom!" I wail.

"I'll be home on Wednesday, honey."

"They're yelling at each other and I have a paper due and I'm pretty sure I smelled *pot* wafting out of Kyle's room."

"We'll talk about it when I get home. You'll be fine."

"Come home *now*!"

If David leaves me alone for more than two days, the kids sprout fangs and grow hair on the backs of their hands, and the bloodletting begins. David has only to re-enter the house and it tilts back to its normal angle of relationship with the ground. Fangs revert magically into teeth, and the kids glide across the floor like well-adjusted machines.

"I need you," I cry.

Most people are afraid their bosses will discover that they are impostors, pretending to have skills they actually lack, simulating a competency they only wish they could claim. But I feel that way at home. Standing helpless before two children who torment each other for entertainment, I am clueless. I have no idea what a good mother looks like.

"Please?" I wheedle my kids. "If you stop fighting, I'll give you ten dollars."

That, thank God, works.

CHAPTER TWELVE

Crying in the Closet

WE LIVE IN BERKELEY.

Have you ever been to Berkeley? Home of the How-Berkeley-Can-You-Be Parade? In which naked people exhort you to strip down and stand up for your rights? In which tiny clowns and enormous dykes and disabled freedom fighters and homeless street people dance to the wild reggae of legally stoned musicians and everyone is laughing, laughing, laughing at how Berkeley we can be? In which cars bedecked with thousands of plastic figurines vie with cars plated in the dragon scales of fractured vinyl records vie with cars sprouting artificial tufts of fuchsia fur? In which the city council hands the Marine Corps' parking place to Code Pink? In which you won't see a Republican bumper sticker within twenty miles but you'll see one asking, *Who would Jesus bomb?*

Or: *Don't believe everything you think.*

Or (Kyle's favorite): *Question Authority.*

Berkeley *is* left field, by definition. Home of the people's right to pee on the sidewalk, impeach the president in a town meeting, and sit in a tree for two years while being immortalized by *News at 5.* Who cares what the rest of the nation thinks? We are Berkeley. We represent the dust on the end of the fringe at the far left of the political spectrum. We vote. You can laugh, but we will be heard, and once you hear us, you will never be safe in your comfortable neighborhood again.

Just kidding.

The reason I bring up Berkeley is because it's necessary to place this story in a context of the liberally insane and permissibly eccentric. Berkeley is the one place where, after gadding about the earth in search of a home, I can finally be myself. You can be whoever you want to be in Berkeley; you can wear outrageous outfits, color your hair any shade you can dream up, and say whatever you think as long as you're not a Republican. I choose to live in a place that embodies acceptance. I am determined to get real.

I finally graduate from psychology school and, since I'm about to become a therapist, figure I'd better get enlightened quick— otherwise, how will I have the credibility to hang out a shingle? I scour the weeklies, passing up Buddhism for Lesbians, Acupuncture for Pets, and Hypnotherapy for Ping-Pong Players, and sign up for a class in shamanism where white middle-class professionals ask their ancestors for career advice while burning sage to cleanse their souls. To further this end, we will all be going on a vision quest.

"What's a vision quest?" I ask the woman sitting next to me. She's scribbling every word the teacher utters into her mandala notebook. The woman ignores me and hunches over a pageful of tiny, cramped epiphanies.

Next, I ask the teacher. She's a smiling Basque woman with a PhD in cultural anthropology, a dispenser of wisdom of international proportions.

"It's a journey into the wilderness," she says, sitting cross-legged at the front of the room. "You'll fast for three days in nature"—she's got to be kidding—"and you will receive a vision. About your life."

I tune out. I'm not going on a vision quest. I slap my notebook closed. I won't be needing notes because I'll be happily ensconced in front of my TV watching *Grey's Anatomy* while the rest of them pick bugs from their teeth. But I am, once again, sorely deluded. As it turns out, the vision quest is not optional. We are all going to the wilderness, including the old and infirm (among whom I tried to include myself in order to exclude myself). And we are going next week.

I pack a backpack with three gallons of water and four gallons of bug juice, and I trudge off with thirty other people to a remote location in the woods where I can pay feverish attention to whatever shows up—which will hopefully not be one of my classmates having a bowel movement. *Is a trail of ants a vision?* I mutter to myself. *Can I go home now?*

We are supposed to notice everything that arises, so I record my observations in a notebook and then try to fall asleep with every creature known to man romping in circles around my head. But of course I can't sleep—sleep is billions of miles away. And while I shiver there all alone with my eyes like headlamps, wondering what the hell I am doing in this godforsaken hellhole, the silence manages to penetrate the chaos of my mind.

Everything gets quiet.

Even my thoughts, riddled with fear, doubt, and anguish, get quiet.

The night is so still that individual sounds ring out like music. And the miracle is that I can hear them. I am actually present enough to hear those heartbreakingly beautiful owl calls and coyote yips without the filter of fear. I can look overhead and glimpse a single star, glimmering like a promise.

Shapes emerge from the darkness, and they are no longer terrifying but luminous, lit by a silvery moon. And as I contemplate how precious moonlight is, how frequently overlooked it is, everything falls into place.

Blam.

It's all connected. Everything (*yes, Cynthia, even that trail of ants*) has a deeper meaning, and everything becomes part of a larger pattern, unraveled before me like a map. My restlessness is connected to my fear is connected to this sudden understanding. I know, for the first time in my life, how to be here. It's not about doing anything, pleasing anyone, performing anything . . . Like the ocean in Hawaii taught me, it's not about struggling. It's about being. Hearing, seeing, sensing, living this one moment the best I can.

Only this. This listening, hunkering, sometimes shivering awareness of the pulse of life all around me, wrapping me up like a warm blanket. The laminate of worry and fear dissolves under the night sky, and I am pure essence: a calm and radiant being made up of five parts silence and ten parts love. Struggle evaporates, and all that remains is awareness as expansive as the night sky. And cuddled inside it, my tiny life. Just a chance expression of the infinite.

My mind, for a change, is utterly still.

I am at peace.

I breathe in, I breathe out. There is nothing to think about.

As I huddle in my sleeping bag under the twinkling sky, listening to the soft tread of river otters returning to their lair, I entertain the possibility of inhabiting this awareness for the rest of my blissful, enlightened life. It's so simple. How could I have missed it? Everything is utterly fine, and I am just a unique particle of the divine. Then I fall asleep, curled on the hard-packed ground, and I dream massive, meaningful, life-changing dreams.

When I wake up, I forget all of it.

"*Mom!*"

"What?"

"Eliza's singing under her breath and I told her to stop."

"I am *not.*"

"You're a piece of cheese stuck on the side of a bus."

"Yeah? Well, you're adopted."

"SILENCE!" I frantically scrabble for the blissful awareness I experienced just five days ago, but all I can find at the back of my mind is a screaming housewife huddled in a broom closet.

"Leave me alone," I shriek, and I stare at my kids with a zombielike expression. Everything I understood is gone. I am gone. There's nothing left in me but panic and freefall. I don't know what to do.

"I am," I say slowly. "Going. Into. My. Room." My voice cracks as I slam my bedroom door and tears fill my eyes. *Why do*

I get so helpless? Why can't I remember the blissful state? Why do I keep forgetting what I must, on some level, deeply know? It feels more painful to forget joy than it was not to have it in the first place.

I decide then and there that I need to permanently install the software that brings me peace of mind. I will take workshops, I will meditate, I will go on as many vision quests as it takes. I will become the prom queen of enlightenment. I will attack this project with all the furor I've ever brought to anything.

But first I will cry in my closet.

"We've had some mountain lion sightings around here," Fritz says, waving a muscled arm across thirty acres of wild land near Cazadero, where I'm about to set up camp. I'm on my third vision quest. Each time I go, I find the peace I seek. Then I instantly forget it when I return to the oil changes, dentist appointments, and client emergencies that are my life. But when I find the peace, it reminds me that I'm part of something bigger, something mystical. I tune in to the cosmic aliveness. Hoping that one day it will stick, like a Varathane sealant on my mental floorboards, I keep heading for the hills.

"If you hear gunshots," Fritz says without expression, "folks are just shooting the lions."

"I hope," I say, swallowing a lump in my throat the size of an apricot, "they don't shoot me."

I trek into the woods and look for a flattish place to unroll my gear. There are none. The playground monitor whispers, *You can't always get what you want.* Fine. I'll sleep on a slope.

After setting up my sleeping bag, I wander through the woods admiring the buttercups that have opened to cup the sunlight and the squirrels that tear across tree limbs playing tag like over-sugared children.

Pay attention to what shows up.

I am content in my silent world, with occasional commentary from the playground monitor. *I've got your back*, she assures me. *Trust me.* Like an idiot, I do.

Darkness falls, and the shadows lengthen and become ominous. The buttercups snap closed, furling their petals against the dark. As the light fades, sounds become aggravating. Soon, in the pitch-blackness of a moonless night, predators begin circling my sleeping bag, the crunch of their footsteps sending shots of adrenaline into my gut.

My eyes are squeezed shut, ensuring that I don't witness horrors that will scar me for life. There are coyotes and wolves and mountain lions out here, circling my head, sniffing my unwashed hair. There are alligators and boa constrictors. They will eat me sooner or they will eat me later, but they will eat me for sure, and my heart is hammering so loudly inside my rib cage that I can barely hear the crackle of their carnivorous steps.

Oh please, I pray to some ill-defined generic god. *Don't let me die.* I take deep, relaxing breaths like my therapist taught me, but my gasps are like those of a drowning person. *Oh please* is all I can say, over and over again, all night long, all 28,800 seconds of it, all 480 minutes, every exacting nanosecond.

By 4:00 a.m., my muscles are yelling from the tension in which they're locked. My head is jackhammering; my heart is a taiko drummer gone berserk, and my eyes are glued shut so tightly I may never be able to pry them open again. *Oh please*, I beg my generic god, unable to even remember what I am praying for. And then, from sheer exhaustion, I give up. *Fine*, I say at last. It is almost 5:00 a.m. and I can't hold on a moment longer.

Fine, fine, fine, fine, fine.

Bring on the mountain lions.

I relax, minimally, at the idea of dying. It couldn't be worse than this. It might actually be a relief. *Kill me now*, I insist with just a touch of melodrama. My throat relaxes enough to allow air to pass through. I inhale a full breath, and my muscles release their convulsive grip.

I am ready to die.

I crack my eyelids, goopy with a night's worth of terror, and I see that the light has grayed and the darkness is fleeing out to sea like a shadowy coward. *Pretend monster*, I scoff. *You old fake.* I see a tree. A normal, kindly tree with perfectly friendly branches hanging over me. Dew on a blade of grass, condensation on my bag. No mountain lions. Birds are beginning to warble.

The night is over.

The rush of relief is so extreme that I feel faint.

That's when I see her. The lion is twenty feet away, bending over the stream, her muscled neck sleek and tawny. I can't breathe. But it isn't fear that stops my breath; it's wonder. She is the most beautiful thing I have ever seen, and I know in that moment that she has come not as a predator to chew on my bones but as a messenger. I sit perfectly still, clutching my sleeping bag around my throat, and stare at the powerful creature. She drinks her fill and then looks up, gazing straight into my eyes, before she swivels on her golden flanks and slides back into the bushes.

The playground monitor takes that moment of silence to whisper, *See?*

I crawl out of my sleeping bag, and I am wrapped in a magical certainty. The mountain lion, because I surrendered to the night, because I survived my terror and finally slowed down to match the pace of my environment, didn't eat me. *Welcome,* she said instead, *to the tempo of the earth.*

I will be slow for several days after I re-enter my ninety-mile-an-hour life thronging with fast cars, fast-food restaurants, and the ability to fast-forward through five hundred brain-deadening TV programs recorded on my TiVo. I will remember the feeling of reverence, the sacred beauty of the lion gazing into my eyes, and I will, for a while, ponder the riddle that threaded itself through my dreams as I tossed and turned under the stars: *How do we let go of fear?*

CHAPTER THIRTEEN

Chocolate Cake All Day

MAMA IS STILL IN SWITZERLAND, FLANKED BY POSSES of concierges, masseurs, bankers, and pedicurists. Children, she feels, are bodies of unrelenting need, so she places large expanses of water between herself and her children and rings us up once a month to air her grievances.

"The White Queen invited me to lunch yesterday," she informs me over the phone. (The White Queen being an expatriate British duchess who lives in the flat below her.) "They are *such* finicky old dykes, and *so* rah-rah the frigging Raj." She heaves a gusty breath through the transatlantic wires. "I'm perfectly happy romping between the sheets with Marcel, though he insists on spending the night. I'm too old for that. It's a good thing I'm so far away, my dear. However would an old woman like me get laid in America?"

She *is* getting older, and we worry about her. One day, as I am eating lunch with my two sisters who have migrated to Berkeley, Judith blurts, "Oh, hell. She can come live with me."

Jill and I spit arugula across the table. Judith hates Mama. Throughout the course of Judith's lifetime, Mama has extemporized on her one unforgivable flaw: she's not thin. People who are not thin, according to Mama, have "let themselves go," and nothing is a greater indicator of slovenliness than a bulging tummy. Judith has borne Mama's displeasure all her life, but she finally managed to escape to Berkeley, land of Be-Who-You-Are, where she trusts that Mama the Etiquette Czar will never deign to set foot.

Wrong.

To our surprise, Mama moves in immediately, tossing her Hermès scarves across the banisters of Judith's house as if she has just bought the place. "Oh," she gushes in a shameless Tallulah Bankhead impersonation. "I'm so glad you invited me. I didn't know if my Swiss bankers would actually change my diapers when the time came."

"Down," barks Judith. "Downstairs. You stay downstairs, Ma. You telephone if you want to come upstairs. And no cooking bacon. That's final."

We keep her in chocolate cake and fresh copies of *The New Yorker*, and Jill finds her a massage therapist who will tickle her clit, so she's as happy as an old harpy can be.

"Don't you think you should eat some vegetables?" I suggest.

"I'm eighty-two years old," she snaps, hunching over her third piece of chocolate cake. "I can finally do what I want."

I bite my lip so I won't utter the truth: she has always done what she wants.

She eats chocolate cake for breakfast, lunch, and dinner and watches soap operas like a junkie. "You'd better leave," she tells me, glancing at her watch. "My soap is on."

We observe her decline with a mixture of fascination and

horror. She gluts on soap operas and enjoys multiple orgasms (while reading Susan Sontag and Stephen Hawking in her spare time), and when she is diagnosed with lung cancer, she flounces into Alta Bates Hospital like visiting royalty, the only Armani wearer in a Value Village Valhalla.

"Those shoes are all wrong," she hisses at an elderly woman attired in sneakers. "Why *must* people dye their hair such unnatural colors?"

Armani-Mom's hair is pure silver. Though she grits her teeth when it starts to gray, she's too much of a purist to dye it, so she flaunts it in a paroxysm of "graceful aging."

"When your hair turns silver," she admonishes us, "you can't wear colors. Only gray, black, or beige. Colors are vulgar."

Here are her regulations:

Never reveal your upper arms.

Get a pedicurist who does house calls.

Get a clit-stimulator who does house calls.

Eat chocolate cake (all day long).

Avoid grandchildren like the plague.

In sum: *If you're tasteful and well-dressed, you can be as insensitive as a yak.*

When the handsome young medic lugs a hospital bed into her room, she croons, "You're the first man to visit me who's brought his own bed!"

As she weakens, though, she softens toward the balding, skeletal creatures who await their toxic dose of chemo at Alta Bates Hospital. "How is your daughter, Maggie?" she asks the fretful mother. "Ellen, you look well today," she lies with astounding sincerity.

"I haven't seen Carl in a few weeks," she comments to a ladder-thin wife. "I hope he hasn't died."

When she abandons the chemo, the doctors prescribe morphine. Our sister Jane flies in from Chicago, and we take turns administering the morphine and changing her diapers. The softening of her personality allows us to love her a little, and we care for her as if she's a large infant with a hyperactive mind.

"We've already done all this," she snaps one day, suddenly awake, four of her daughters sprawled on the bed around her. "Why are we doing it again?"

"You're dying, Ma," I tell her, wondering what kind of morphine déjà vu she's having.

"Oh, that," she says, looking bored. Then she narrows a glassy eye, revealing a twinkle of mischief. "I'm considering the alternatives."

If anyone can find an alternative, Armani-Mom can.

But she continues to deteriorate, and finally, she sinks into a coma. Her very last words emerge from her comatose lips when a visiting nurse makes a fatal mistake.

"In order to give you your bath," the nurse clucks with efficient cheer, "we're going to roll you over so you can lay on your left side."

Oops. Even in her coma, the Grammar Nazi twitches. There's a pause in the universe, as if the planets have ceased spinning just for a moment. As time stands still over my mother's pale and unresponsive body, awaiting the wrath only she can muster, she slits a reptilian eye and glares at the nurse. "It's not *lay*," she whispers. "It's *LIE!*"

Then she dies.

On June 5, 2001, with four of her daughters arrayed around her stick-bone body like East, West, North, and South, Elizabeth Teague spits up her ghost. We brush her silver hair and wash her rice-paper skin and dress her in her favorite Missoni kaftan. We light candles and sage and say prayers from three different belief systems, and we know she's left her body when the cat crouches beside her empty shell and yowls a dirge that curls our arm hairs. To see her lying there, blue and cold, grips our hearts. Her reign is over. The four of us join hands in begrudging respect for the monolithic personality that has just departed the earth.

My ailing dad, on the other hand, withdraws into a fortress of his own making. His fourth wife, the perfectly Botoxed Barbie chosen to lionize him at dinner parties, denies us access. "You'll only upset him," she tells us.

She keeps us, the rabid, emotional hordes, at bay. She shoots us an email when he dies. It's 2003.

We sit at his memorial service, surrounded by the wailing students he supported through college, the civic officials he bribed, and the government mucky-mucks who all revered the great globe-trotting Harry Moore. Hell, the Queen of England decorated him in person. We, his children, adored him, too, but it was no substitute for love. He was a rock star up on stage, the lights too bright for him to see us down below. At the end of his life, unable to keep up the performance, he slunk away to an inaccessible place where, alone in his bed, he released his last breath.

He couldn't bear for the world to see him fail.

Engraved notice sent to the papers. Children notified. Game over.

I miss him terribly, with a grinding ache in my gut. But I had the same ache when he was alive, so what have I lost? The longing?

It's still there.

CHAPTER FOURTEEN

Closet Drama Queen

IT TURNS OUT THAT SHARON, MY THREE O'CLOCK, HAS LOST her father, too. She snuffles into a fistful of tissues, and I allow her time to process her grief. "You give me permission to feel it," she says, causing me—I admit—to preen just a little. "You've really helped," she adds.

I inflate.

"Can I call you while you're on vacation?"

Just as quickly, I deflate.

Here's the part no one tells you about being a therapist: therapists are rife with contradictions. First of all, we *love* being needed. We eat it up like monsters gobbling cookies on afternoon TV. *Need me*, we say to our poor, beleaguered clients, though we would never admit it. But we also feel trapped. Hence: *Don't need me. Don't call me on weekends. I truly care about you—now pay me.*

It's a business wrought from paradox. *I'm totally here for you, but only on Wednesdays.*

I look at Sharon and my frozen expression melts. "You just lost your father," I say gently. "You're trying to figure out what holds your world together."

She blows her nose.

"I'll only be gone for a week," I continue in a soft tone. "You're going to be okay until I get back."

Sharon straightens her spine and takes a breath. "I know," she says. "It was worth a try."

I am getting better at listening, better at reading my clients' body language, and better at following them into the dark corners that frighten them. I pay attention to what they're not telling me, and I meet them exactly where they are. I am *doing less*.

I sit up and observe Sharon's gestures, noting her listless appearance. She tells me that her grief is so all-consuming that she feels disconnected from herself. She's having trouble with her children, who run roughshod over her at home.

"When do you feel most connected with yourself?" I ask her.

"When I'm teaching," she says. "It fills me with a kind of power and confidence I don't have anywhere else."

"Can you sense that in your body?"

"Yes."

I ask her to close her eyes. "How would it feel to carry that confidence home with you, where you feel so powerless?" I whisper.

Sharon breathes deeply, imagining her confident self entering her home, confronting her unruly children. Her lips twist, and she laughs out loud. "I would stand up for myself," she says. "I wouldn't be such a goddamn pussy around my kids."

Ka-blam.

It's uncanny how they hold up the mirror you don't want to see.

I'm also a pussy around my kids, I don't tell her.

Sharon writes out her check while I tactfully gaze out the window. "Thank you so much," she says, handing me the check. I accompany her to the door and feel a blaze spreading through my chest. Not because I have helped her, which is lovely, but because she has given me something invaluable.

Each client is a mirror, showing us the work that we need to do, and Sharon has reminded me that I need to empower myself as a mother. I've been hobbled by insecurity. I will take this lesson home with me and try to grow a backbone with my kids.

As I open the door to see her out, I think of all the dramas that play in therapists' heads as we blink and nod behind the glass of our unassailable neutrality. It's the ultimate acting job. Because underneath that placid exterior, we are bubbling away in our own stink, working on our issues right alongside our clients. We may look calm, but we're actually closet drama queens, every one of us, laboring away in the smoke-belching factories of our own unconscious.

I close the door and fall into my chair.

The minute I get home, I am assailed by the inner fascist that requires me to be a combination of Julia Child, Donatella Versace, and Mother Teresa, dispensing necessary tips on how to survive a hostile world while setting the perfect dinner table for thirty.

It's Christmas vacation, the time when good mothers cook and clean and force unwanted consumer goods down their families' throats like rabid fairy godmothers while stirring impossible French sauces and extolling the virtues of thank-you cards.

My kids are out of school for the holiday break, and the good mother superego is a many-tentacled squid crushing me in her fishy arms. I clutch my Christmas list in one hand while I listen to emergency voicemails from clients, and my brain is short-circuiting like a flap-zapping electrical wire. I escape downstairs to seize a quick therapeutic conversation with my friend Deb.

"I had a nightmare in which you were pregnant again, wearing an apron like *I Love Lucy.*" She laughs. "I was trying to talk to you, and you couldn't understand a word I was saying."

"Exactly," I say. "That's exactly what's happening right now, and I can't understand a word you're saying. What's your name again?"

"Okay, listen," says Deb, adopting her no-nonsense voice. "This will last exactly two weeks, and you will think you've lost every shred of sanity, but you haven't. You're just in holiday mode."

"Oh, great," I say. "Holiday mode makes me sociopathic. What kind of a mother am I?"

"You're a fine mother. You just can't be a mother and yourself at the same time."

"Oh."

"Call me after Christmas," she says.

Who I am not, I think in a sulk as I burn the Christmas cookies, *is Katie Jackson.*

Katie Jackson is a new friend from the lake who tosses off a perfect dinner for fifty in her spare time, arranging it on hand-thrown plates while entertaining her guests with scintillating observations about neo-capitalist economies. Katie Jackson has dinner parties for lawyers from unpronounceable countries while whipping out immaculate desserts. I envy her enough to kill her in a uniquely creative way. Mince? Julienne? Poach on a bed of arugula? She will just pop back up with her *Bon Appétit* smile intact and inquire if I need another cocktail.

I invite her to dinner over the holiday. She takes in my dé-cor—plastic soccer trophies and chipped ceramic rhinoceroses made by my children in fits of artistic verve—with a bemused expression. "Your house is so . . . *homey*," she says, heading for the wine.

I've ordered takeout because I am so afraid that if I go anywhere near the stove while Katie Jackson is in my house, I will set myself on fire, and the guests, mistaking my flaming torso for something *flambé*, will take a carving knife to my haunch. "I got new flatware," I announce, desperate to impress. Katie blinks at me and fills her glass.

Later that night, lying in bed next to David, I shudder to remember my more embarrassing moments. That's when I realize that I don't hate Katie Jackson. I want to *be* Katie Jackson. She is everything a mother should be: she is Donna Reed and Doris Day and Martha Stewart with a dash of Christiane Amanpour thrown in. I study her as an anthropologist would study a Sulawesian tribe, hoping her perfection will somehow rub off on me.

The next day, manically mimicking Katie Jackson, I whip up some aioli, scrub the kitchen, vacuum the cat, and give myself a

pedicure in case Kyle and Eliza should catch sight of—*gasp!*—
my horned toes. When I casually offer them a dish of aioli, they
look at me as if I am someone's demented grandmother.

The thing is, I can't tell my children that no one taught me
how to be a mother. No one taught me to bake pies or sew buttons or fricassee a rabbit. I pretend I'm Supermom, who never
doubts, never has bad breath, and never worries that her breasts
are full of lumps. I have to smile and produce—*voilà!*—a perfect
meal while folding their laundry and changing the sheets on
their smelly beds.

I stare at my children and my eyes fill with tears while I
imagine myself shrinking, shrinking, shrinking into a little girl
who doesn't have a clue how real mothers are supposed to behave.
*I was raised in a finishing school, for God's sake. I learned French
and macramé and curse words in Hebrew.* I gaze at my beloved
children and my body curves in apology.

But then I remember my client Sharon, who walked her
powerful self right into her home and stood up to her kids. She
pretended to believe in herself until she did. She took charge
and became the mother she was meant to be.

I can do that.

"Kids," I say, with wobbly newfound strength in my voice,
"I'm not too sure what a good mother looks like, but I'm going
to start setting some boundaries around here." I take a breath,
praying I won't be struck by lightning.

When their faces crease into grins, happiness burns a hole in
my heart.

"Mom," says Kyle. "It's about time."

CHAPTER FIFTEEN

Mutation Blues

EVEN THOUGH I HAVE QUIT THE THEATER, I STILL TEACH
drama to twelve-year-olds. Every year, as the drama teacher for a
private school in Berkeley, I write a play for the specific eccen-
tricities of my sixth-grade class, setting wacky characters into a
sociopolitical satire complete with a musical score and rousing
songs.

"Jamie, will you *stop* climbing on the desks? It's your line."

"Cynthia"—*snurfle*—"my cat died!"

"Oh, Danny, I'm sorry. That's really rough. But can you get
into place for your entrance? This is dress rehearsal."

This year's play is *The Mutation Blues*. Dayglo Canyon Nuclear Power Plant has suffered a meltdown and the citizenry is
mutating: some have three arms while others have two heads
or four rows of teeth set in permanent, bleached smiles, and
the local politicians' brains have—surprise!—mutated into
prehistoric sludge. The young actress who plays Sally Spokes-
clone is at this moment sprinting down the hall, screaming.

"Sally!" I yell, smelling the burnt rubber of my sizzling nerve
endings. Directing kids is like herding chickens—they are never

where they're supposed to be. So I pull out my annual That's-It-I-Quit routine. I take a deep breath and hurl my script to the floor with a satisfying *thwack* and thunder, "THAT'S IT—I QUIT!"

This shuts them up. If I quit, they can't perform, and really, they've endured years of math and science and art and English with the understanding that in sixth grade, they can Be In The Play. Being In The Play is what gives their lives meaning. Or, at any rate, major goofing-off time.

"I can't work with you all running around like cockroaches on crack. I want professional attitudes and professional cues and professional line readings because this is a professional production. We are going into a real theater, and you will be paid real money." (It's approximately $8 per person, but what the hell.) "I want professional behavior out of each and every one of you, or I'm out of here."

Silence. Forty-four eyes round as twenty-two twelve-year-olds goggle at me. They stop horsing around and pay perfect attention for the rest of the day, and we get through dress rehearsal.

The following night, five minutes before curtain, Joey Black can't find his pants, Elsa Leibner forgets her lines, Beth Buckley calls in sick, and Billy Mellon ties his shoelaces together.

"This is a knot," I cry, panic curdling my voice as I hear the crowds of people settling into their seats, expecting the curtain to rise any minute. "I can't get this undone!"

"I know," Billy wails.

"It's time," whispers Mark, my composer/piano player. "Should I open the curtain?"

"NO!" I shriek, still scrabbling with Billy's shoelaces, imagining in my frenzy the direst of solutions: chop off the laces, chop off the shoes, chop off his feet! But in a blinding flash of clear-sightedness, it hits me. At this critical moment just before curtain on opening night, the star of my play has tied his own shoes together in a knot, and if that's not funny, what is? I start to chuckle. Billy joins in, and soon Mark is laughing, too. While the three of us giggle like maniacs, I whiz through that knot and hoist myself off the floor.

"Let's get this show on the road."

Billy scrambles into position, the curtain is raised, and twenty-one voices soar in perfect unself-conscious harmony:

> *I went to the doctor just the other day.*
> *I said I feel kind of weird. He said go away.*
> *My head felt strange. My body was in traction.*
> *Didn't know I was the victim of a chemical reaction.*
> *I've got the blues*
> *Na Na Na Na*
> *Blues*
> *Na Na Na Na*
> *I've got the Dip Dip Dip Dip*
> *Ma Ma Ma Ma*
> *Mutation blues.*

They are a miracle of class-act showmanship, delivering every comic beat, every pause, every piece of stage business. Belting out their lines like pros, they sing, dance, and act their way to a thunderous ovation. Each child is a star: the clowns crash into the walls, the bombasts bellow, and the politicians pontificate. It's a wonder to behold.

As I watch from the wings, gnawing my knucklebones, I know that it will never get better than this: the pure joyful abandon of twelve-year-olds on a stage. Their songs shake the rafters, making up in glee what they lack in harmony. The audience laughs so hard the bleachers rattle. For all those kids, for their families, and even for the English teachers and gym teachers and science teachers, these two nights where twenty-two kids become, for sixty-odd minutes, translucent, are worth all the daily struggles of our lives. Time stops. While searching for acclaim in all the wrong places, I have happened to create, almost by accident, this ecstatic experience in my community. Even if I can't bring myself to perform anymore, I can still make theater. For one moment, unencumbered by my own thwarted needs, I have made magic.

While I'm teaching kids and building my private psychotherapy practice, I finish my novel. I closet myself every morning in my downstairs study and hammer away at the computer until I finally spit out a book. It's an act of spontaneous ejaculation.

What, I think, *just happened?*

My first novel is a coming-of-age story about a twelve-year-old girl with an abusive mother. She is assaulted by men before she's able to heal and find her real self. It's a story I will have to tell again and again, ad nauseam, but one day, I hope, I will tell a different story.

Soon I have an agent for my novel. She's talking to New

York publishers, and my fantasies of cheap glory spring back to life. *Oprah, here I come.*

But the publishers prevaricate, and hope, like a roller coaster, soars and dips as they consider my book, then reject it. "It won't sell," they tell me. "You're a good writer. Why don't you write a blockbuster?"

Hahaha.

I keep writing. The clattering of my fingers on the keyboard fills my lungs with air. Writing gives expression to my huddled and hidden inside self. I write two more (non-blockbuster) novels and send them to my agent, praying to all the gods of cultural approbation to help me just this once. I want to be published so badly that my gums hurt. While I ache for acclaim, my playground monitor clucks in the background like a peevish chicken.

Rejection letters pile up.

I absorb the rejections and plow along, improving as I go. Soon, I am 75 percent more literate than I was before. Instead of crashing and burning, I'm learning from my failures.

Failure becomes my teacher.

I don't turn away from the pain. I feel it and move on. I try to write better, be more real with each book. I am trying to find my voice, and it isn't the voice that shouts in competition with men, seeking approval. It's a quieter, more honest voice; it's a feminine voice, and I barely know her. I read hundreds of books, stoke the furnace of my love, and keep on writing.

Writing peels away the skin of driving ambition. Writing becomes my meditation practice. Writing is what I love.

CHAPTER SIXTEEN

The Truth Reverberates like a Gong

"YOU FAILED ME, CYNTHIA."

It's Bonnie, a quaking leaf of a woman who has been seeing me for six months. "I asked you to call me on my birthday and you didn't."

I am stunned. I don't call clients unless it's an emergency, and I would never have scheduled a social call, even on someone's birthday. This adherence to strict rules of behavior with clients is called the *frame*, and it guarantees consistent boundaries. Basically, it assures clients that their therapist won't drop in for dinner or attend their cat's cremation. I may waffle around my children, but I keep clear boundaries with my clients. (I've come a long way since the days of playing gin rummy with my Wednesday client.)

"What do you remember about that conversation, Bonnie? Let's figure out what happened."

"You promised to call because I might get depressed."

I never would have—

"I can't trust you anymore."

Here we go. Sometimes, as therapists, we have to take on a projection—in other words, we become someone's abusive mother or husband. When this happens, we can help clients explore the role they've cast us in. Arguing with the legitimacy of their projection is counterproductive.

"Tell me," I say gently, "what it's like not to trust me."

Bonnie has regressed to a six-year-old now, flashing back to her aunt Margaret, who lied to her. "I'm so mad," she says, curling into herself.

I can't help but notice the double message between her words and her body language. I take a deep breath and drop my shoulders, which have clenched around my neck. *You can handle this*, I remind myself, trying not to relive the terror induced by my stepfather's rage.

"How does it feel to be mad at me, Bonnie?" Shaking off the past, I deliberately focus on the woman in front of me.

"If you cared, you would have called me."

I force my jaw to relax. "It feels like nobody cares?"

"Yeah." She sniffs into her tissue.

"I'm sorry you're hurting, Bonnie." I exhale. "Let's see if we can work this out together. What do you want to say to me?"

"I want you to feel bad."

I pull air into my constricted lungs. "You want me to feel your pain." I'm relieved to note that my voice is calm and soft.

"I hate you," she explodes. She looks excited, as though she's blurted something she's been dying to say for years.

"Keep going, Bonnie. You hate me right now."

"Yeah. I hate how you treat me. How everybody treats me! I'm *sick* of not mattering."

There is a moment in therapy when the truth is spoken and

it reverberates throughout the room like a gong. I am silent, and Bonnie hears her truth echoing around us.

"You're sick of not mattering," I repeat gently.

"Yeah."

"What do you want to say to all of us who have made you feel you don't matter?" I ask.

"I need you to consider me! I'm not a piece of furniture," she snaps, surprising herself with her own vehemence. Her spine has uncurled and she sits up straight on the couch for the first time that day.

"Thank you for telling me that," I say, flooded with respect for her in that moment.

Bonnie exhales a huge breath, and I give her a moment to feel the import of what she has said.

"You've been storing that up for years," I tell her. "How did it feel to let it out?"

"It felt great," she says, blowing her nose.

Later, we will talk about how to express her anger more skillfully, but for now, allowing it to be voiced is enough.

"It felt amazing to have you hear it without rejecting me."

"I'm honored by your trust, Bonnie."

"Thank you."

I'm growing up. A little bit at a time.

I volunteer my therapy services at a homeless shelter, and the first time I walk across the threshold of that battered place, something collapses inside me like a falling building.

I walk into the common room, which is filled with heavy-browed single men and grimy barefoot children corralled by expressionless mothers whose eyes have seen the collapse of Western civilization from up close. These are the people we have shoved off the lifeboat, the drowning souls we force to sleep on our streets, in our doorways. Their blank gaze accuses me of inhumanities I cannot bear to own, and standing on that threshold, I feel privileged, terrified, and way too white.

"I'm Janie," says a bright-faced woman in a flowered smock. She seems to be the self-appointed spokeswoman for the residents who are attending this group session. "We're so glad you're here."

I suspect they have been urged to come to this group to fulfill a requirement rather than because they want a therapy session with a charitably minded provider.

"I thought you might like to try some guided meditation," I stammer once we have organized ourselves into a ragtag circle of chairs. "Have any of you ever tried meditation?"

"Of course we have," snaps an angry-looking mother of two. "Do you think we're clueless?"

"Cynthia!" calls Marjo, the director of the shelter, striding through the door. "Let me introduce everyone."

I meet Betty and Shareen and Claudetta and Dawne and Magda and JoEllen and Keesha. I ask them to close their eyes and imagine a safe place. Dawne whispers that her safe place is under her bed. Her drunk daddy is coming into her room. That's when I realize that these women don't have a safe place. They can't even imagine one. A hole yawns in my belly.

So instead, I invite them to imagine a garden where they can smell the flowers, feel the sun on their skin, and hear a stream running nearby. I suggest that they follow a path until they find a wise old woman sitting on a bench. They can ask her anything they want. I give them some time.

When they open their eyes, half of them say they can't imagine a woman like that, and the other half tell me they can't picture a garden. My heart clenches into a fist. *I have nothing to offer these women.*

That's when I decide to just listen. Carl Rogers said that listening is the greater part of therapy. I need to meet these women where they are and stop trying to take them somewhere else. I need to learn from them.

"What's it like here?" I ask them, leaning forward on my plastic chair. I really want to know.

"I've never had this kind of support before," says a tiny, frail woman who is cradling her two-year-old. The child, for some reason, has not uttered a sound. "It's hard to believe people care, but they do. If I can finally get strong enough to get my own housing, I'll be on my own again, and that's scary."

Another woman with silver dreadlocks says, "Out on the street, you don't have a door you can close. The first time I closed the door to my room here at the shelter, I cried."

Several women nod in agreement.

"We fight, though," admits Claudetta. "We fight over the TV and the potato chips and the shampoo. Sometimes women can be real bitches."

"Do you feel angry a lot?" I venture.

More nodding.

"Sometimes it's easier to feel angry than it is to feel sad," I say.

"Not safe to feel sad," agrees a large, quiet woman named Magda.

There is rustling in the room as women move restlessly in their chairs.

"Could we go around the room and name one positive thing you want the other people in this circle to know about you?"

"I have a big heart," says Dawne.

"I'm real strong," says Magda.

"I love my babies."

"I'll knock you down if you hurt my friends." They all laugh.

Betty says, "I'll tell you the truth if you want to hear it or not!"

Everyone relaxes. Their posture is less tense, and I'm no longer curled up in my chair.

"I nursed a man on the street I didn't even know," whispers Shareen. "He didn't have nobody else to take care of him."

"I'm gonna get me a place to live," says Claudetta. "I'm gonna have a shower and a potted plant and two locks on the door."

"I'm just waiting for God to hear my prayers," Keesha says in a voice that's more like a whisper. The silence feels bottomless. My eyes fill with tears.

"Okay, then," I say, picking up my purse. "I'll come back next week if you want to do this again."

"We do," they say.

I exhale, grateful for their warmth. "Thank you," I say. I look each woman in the eye. My cheeks burn and I swallow the hypocrisy of charity, in which we come to give but end up taking instead. I thought I had something to offer these women, and that was a lie.

"For what?" JoEllen asks.

"For reminding me of the most important gift we can give one another: how to listen."

CHAPTER SEVENTEEN

I'm Enlightened, Goddammit!

I HAVE TWO BEAUTIFUL KIDS, A GREAT HUSBAND, AND A thriving practice. Working with clients is a continual discovery.

I watch Eileen, who sits slumped on the couch. Usually a bubbly extrovert, full of ideas and abuzz with activities, she is despairing. She keeps changing her career, but she can't find "the right job."

"I get so overwhelmed when I look at Craigslist," she says, "I want to die."

"Tell me what happens," I say.

Eileen closes her eyes. "I feel like I'm going crazy," she muses. "There's too much information. The *shoulds* pile up and I get panicky."

"What happens in your body?"

"I feel like I'm moving through cement. I'm frozen, and there's a brick lodged in my chest."

Damn, I think, making rapid calculations about how much time we have left. Trauma shows up in one of four ways: fight, flight, freeze, or collapse. When a client is frozen, it takes time to unlock.

"Tell me about feeling frozen." I eye the clock.

Eileen struggles visibly for a moment, then says, "I feel stuck."

"Okay," I say. "What's that like?"

"I don't know," she says. "It's like all the lights have gone out. There's nobody home." Underneath trauma is a terrifying vacancy, an utter absence of self. I know this place too well.

"That's scary," I say softly.

Eileen nods.

Twelve minutes, I think, *to get the lights back on.*

"What's underneath that?" I blurt. "If the stuckness is there to keep you from feeling something deeper, what is it?"

The clock ticks forward in time, and Eileen starts to cry. "I feel nauseous," she says at last, grabbing the tissues I hand her. *Nauseated*, the Grammar Nazi snarls, and I push her away, leaning forward.

"Nauseous is good," I say. "You're at an edge."

"It's scary." She buries her face in the Kleenex. "Like I'm flying into pieces."

"Uh-huh," I say. "Flying into pieces." *No longer frozen.*

"Feels like I'm gonna die."

"I'll bet that goes way back."

"Yeah," she admits. "When I was four years old, I'd get this feeling." Tears sluice down her face; the stuckness has cracked open to expose grief. She is in the original wound.

"That," I say gently, "is what's underneath your depression." We sit in silence while she takes this in. "What's the belief?" I ask.

"No one is here to help me."

"No one," I say quietly, "was there to help you when you were four and that little girl felt like she would die."

"Yeah."

"Like she would fly apart."

A tiny whisper, "Yeah . . ."

"But she didn't die. She survived."

Eileen shudders.

"Is anyone helping you now?"

"Yes, lots of people are helping me." She sits up, her eyes still closed. "My husband, my sister, you." She inhales. "I get it." She opens her eyes. "I need to love that four-year-old part of me, to help her when she's scared."

"That's it," I say softly.

I gaze out the window as she writes her check, trying to keep my stomach from growling like an eighteen-wheeler. When Eileen leaves, I take my sandwich from the mini-fridge, and as I eat, I think about my own inner four-year-old, who has tried all her life to be better than she is. To be someone else. Someone lovable. A huge sadness wells up in me, and I see her sitting across from me. I send her a wave of love and say, *You're okay. You're a good person.* I blink. *I'll take care of you.*

The tears come unexpectedly. I sit there for a long time, staring at the empty couch.

Still thinking that if I could just get enlightened, I'd be a better therapist and a more effective mother—and, okay, maybe a little happier—I go see this guy, Adyashanti, who's giving a talk in Oakland. Adyashanti is supposed to be an "awakened being," and I want to see what that looks like. Specifically in a twenty-first-century person in blue jeans, a buzz cut, and a blazer. What it looks like is a house that's been burgled. The guy's eyes are as empty as an Arizona sky.

He sits in a chair on a wooden stage, his expression smooth and unruffled. Imagine a monk's cell with nothing in it, except maybe a slant of crooked light, or a mote of dust. No, not even a mote of dust. His eyes are as clean as Windexed glass. Next to him, I feel like an attic crammed with belongings from a hundred years ago, collecting mold, teetering in piles, threatening an avalanche to anyone stupid enough to open the door. All the stuff I have ever thought about, worried about, fretted or wept about, is lying there in stacks, rotting, while Adyashanti's room is sparkling clean and bare.

When he looks out at the auditorium filled with desperate seekers who cling to his every word, he gazes impassively through those empty eyes. You can tell he's seeing exactly what's there. He's not seeing his own projections, his past failures, his future hopes. You have no idea what it would be like to see what's there, because your own lenses are so damn spotty with preconceptions. What actually is just there, if you could see it? The hum of eternity? The white light of bliss?

I try to imagine it: seeing the world from the empty room of my brain. There would be no fear, no striving. I would hear sounds and smell smells without the filter of my thoughts, and I would be utterly present. I have tasted this on my vision quests. My gaze relaxes and I settle into my seat.

The more I listen to this guy who doesn't have a stick of furniture in his rooms, the more blissful I feel. It's as if I can mimic his state just by watching him, and pretty soon, my own furniture melts away and I'm as clean as a bare closet. Maybe

I'm a tiny bit enlightened. I listen to questions from the audience, feeling superior, and I glance at Adyashanti to remind myself that he doesn't even have a stick of superiority in his bare room. He doesn't even have—and I gulp with vertigo at this thought—walls. Not even a floor. Not even a room, really, to tell the truth. There is no self left. If that's enlightenment, maybe I don't want it after all.

Rooting in my purse for my car keys, I speed home, dodging semis and smart cars, thinking about those empty eyes. Nothing. No mothers, no fathers, no thoughts, no platforms, no identities. Freedom. And everything, for just a brief flap of an eyelid, gets really quiet. Everything pauses. There is no thought. I'm driving along Interstate 580, and I have this unquenchable sensation of joy. I'm not even out in the wilderness, where it usually happens; I'm right here on Interstate 580 speeding through Oakland. Everything that torments me has evaporated, and I'm at one with the fundamental ease that is the heart of the universe.

I want to yell, *I've got it!* I want to crank down my window and holler, *I'm enlightened, goddammit!* My personal narrative has dissolved, and I exhale into a world so squeaky-clean, all that's left is love.

I take a breath of that crystal silence, and then, before I can exhale, the machinery roars back into life like a city coming out of a blackout. All the lights flip on and the CD player resumes its nasty, pounding beat. Horns, cranky drivers, subways thundering underfoot. All the stories retrieve their narratives, including my own—and my thoughts are once again a crowd of junkies on a street corner trying to sell me their version of my life.

I slowly exhale and put on my blinker to take the Fifty-First

Street exit, and a guy in a Ford pickup cuts me off. Honking, I veer around him as my heart rate hits 160. *Asshole.*

Enlightenment—*sigh*—comes and goes.

My friend Paul, in the voice of a thirteen-year-old with his first Fender bass, tells me he's bought a helmet that will stimulate his happiness nodes.

"It's so cool," he enthuses. "You wear it every day for an hour and it makes you happy."

Is that what I'm after? Being happy? It's a layer of it, for sure. But there's another layer of it that runs even deeper, which is not feeling happy, and that's okay, too.

"At the center of me," says the Buddha, "is a clear pool that cannot be disturbed, no matter what happens outside me. This is my vow to myself and to all sentient beings: I will sit, one hand on the earth as my witness, and let every manner of suffering, temptation, and obligation parade before my eyes, and I will not give up this seat, which is my only certainty. I sit, I breathe, I observe, and the world passes through the empty room of my awareness without taking hold."

You get it and then you lose it. But the thing is, when you get it for just a moment, you are suffused with a feeling of love so sharp that it takes your breath away. As if every table, every chair, every butterfly is an expression of love. Even the angry man in the next car: love. The uncertainty and the scrambling and the restlessness and the doubt: love. My children, my husband, my clients, my friends: the gently smiling faces of love.

This is, after all is said and done . . . a love story.

CHAPTER EIGHTEEN

Hot Rod Rodeo

"I DON'T HAVE ANY C-CELL BATTERIES UP HERE IN THE mountains," says David. He's finished reconstructing our cabin on the lake, and this is his excuse for not hanging up the cat clock with the wagging eyes and flapping tail I gave him for our tenth wedding anniversary. I love that clock. I had one just like it when I was a child. Does David love the cat clock? *NO.* It's still moldering in its box while David performs duties of questionable necessity at our mountain cabin and I am having a mini-breakdown back at home.

"It's fine," I say in the muffled voice of a practiced martyr. My throat has swelled up, all itchy and throbbing like it gets when I eat cantaloupe, and I suppress the urge to sneeze. This is what happens when I lie.

"Okay," says David, and I think, *Our marriage is over.*

I get like this sometimes. All women do. It's called *Get This Right or It's Over.* It's the moment when twenty years of minor transgressions loom into cataclysmic proportion and love is utterly lost. Let me explain: David has read only one book in the past ten years. Was it *Crime and Punishment* or *Bleak House*?—because those I could forgive—No.

It was *Hot Rod Rodeo.*

David's idea of culture is Monday Night Football. *Grounds for divorce.* (I know you agree.) David has grease under his fingernails and a concretistic view of the world that brooks no mysticism while I burn for dark, neurotic communion about Nietzsche. I am wild with grass-is-goddamn-greener-itis.

"It's okay," I say, even though it isn't. "I'll take it back." I pronounce those same four words every Christmas when David doesn't like the Gore-Tex rain pants, the Waterpik, or the fleece slippers I bought him. Then I grit my teeth and paw through my wallet for the receipt. Every year, I take his present back and tell myself it doesn't rankle.

"Here's Kyle." I quickly hand the phone off before saying something I'll regret.

While David and Kyle ramble on about motor oil and carburetor leaks and other moronic man things, I swelter. I clench my teeth and fulminate. "End of marriage," I mutter. "I'm so out of here."

"Dad wants to talk to you," Kyle says in the phlegmatic monotone that only teenagers can affect, and after a pause to catch my breath, I take the phone.

"I asked Kyle to bring me some C-cell batteries when he comes up," says David. The pause between us deepens into a Grand Canyon of hope. "For the cat clock," he finishes.

My heart-gates open and blood floods into my vena cava. My throat relaxes, and all the bitchy comments retreat to wherever bitchy comments retreat to—probably my armpit.

"I love the cat clock," he says.

I take a breath, and sunshine pours through the window like melted butter. I adore this man.

"You do?" I ask in a small voice, grateful to have escaped the ignominy of divorce lawyers and division of property yet again.

"I *love* it," he avows. "Now, when are you coming up here? I need you to bring my air compressor."

When I arrive at the cabin, my beloved cat clock hangs over the refrigerator, wagging its tail and rolling its eyes like a bad Kabuki actor. David is waiting for me with the eager expression of a puppy dog about to be taken on a walk. We stroll across every surface of the terrain that surrounds our beloved lake. We swim, we bike, we drink wine on the deck overlooking the water, and we make love in the morning, remaining shamelessly in bed until ten o'clock. *This is good for you*, I tell myself. *Now shut up.*

Because here's the thing: whenever I take a vacation, my mind informs me that a moment without striving will delete all my hard-earned skills and render me incapable of functioning. My mind loves tales of dread and woe. Legends of decapitation and dismemberment and death, especially at 3:00 a.m.

For example:

You will become boring, all your friends will abandon you, and you'll die alone.

I sigh. I get up and lie down. I eat crackers. I watch my mind run around the room like an un-housebroken puppy crapping on the nylon carpet, and I say, in a compassionate, therapeutic tone, "You are feeling insecure right now, and that's understandable, but don't be contaminating my vacation with your neurotic horseshit."

Stunned into silence, my mind pauses before escalating in volume. *You will lose your clients and your mind (that's me), and they will lock you up in a small room with mattresses on the walls.*

"I'm going back to bed. You can't scare me."

"Oh, no? What about that lump in your left breast?"

I leap into my bed and yank the covers over my head. This is the family posture. From my oldest sister Judith all the way down the line, we are most comfortable deep in the boats of our beds with the covers drawn over our heads like great deflated sails. Thus cocooned, we wait wide-eyed for a gust of wind to sweep us away to a new continent where no one suffers from imaginary ailments like insanity.

Later, as David and I lie on the dock watching motorboats drag humans through the water in a parade of alarming contortions, I catch him peering at me from the corner of his eye. I know this look. He's wondering if I'm enjoying this, if I'm actually able, for this brief moment in time, to stop perseverating long enough to fall in love with a mountain, to laugh at a duck. *Is she working herself into a tizzy?* he's thinking. *Will she ever be able to relax and smell the outboard motors?*

No.

I'm sorry, I really am, but I hate vacations. Here's my thinking: if you don't work every day, sweating and grunting over some impossible cause, throwing yourself headfirst at cinderblock walls, you'll be trampled by competing armies when Armageddon blasts everyone into smithereens. Or something.

I'd rather be working.

I've got things to do, people to be, epitaphs to earn. I've got to go home and get enlightened. No one gets enlightened around motorboats.

I paste a tragic smile on my face and climb into my car. *I'm going back to work*, I yodel as I drive into Berkeley, clomp up the stairs to my office, and sink with a sigh into my chair. *Ahh*, I think.

Bring on the neurotic hordes.

CHAPTER NINETEEN

The Art of Flying

I HAVE A FULL THERAPY PRACTICE BY NOW, BUT IN THE mornings, when the kids are at school, I still go downstairs, sit in front of my keyboard, and write.

I stare at the dripping rain on the windowpanes, and calm, like a cloud of incense, wraps itself around me. I know exactly what will happen next, and it is the one thing that makes me feel truly whole.

The stories come, barreling along like cars on a freeway, headlights on bright, honking and passing and tailgating and sometimes running out of gas. I love them. They are my cantankerous children, and I try to be good to them and find each one of them a home, although some of them have to be snipped, which always hurts. When the stories come, they call me to life.

As a child, I clutched my sweaty pencil and scratched words into dog-eared composition books while my stepfather bellowed at my mother. The louder he yelled, the faster I wrote. I had to drown out his voice and all the demons he released into our house, and I could do it only by writing. I wrote until he went to bed and my heart stopped racketing in my chest. I wrote about people who were predictable and kind, and those words became the home I never had.

This is why I'm a therapist: I get to listen to stories all day long. I never know what the story will be or how it will end. I sit in my therapist's chair like a child at her grandmother's knee, breathless as I wait for the unraveling of my client's personal trajectory through a flea-bitten life of disappointment and heartbreak, a story no writer could invent.

Or I sit, like now, at my keyboard, and my own story unfolds itself like a peacock's tail. The characters run out in the rain and lose their minds or go to nursing school and die, and they make me laugh and cry.

If I didn't have stories, life would be too hard.

Richard calls.

He's a friend from my Hawkeye days. He's writing a book, and he wants to tell me all about it. Gritting my teeth, I agree to meet him for coffee.

Richard is a beanpole with frizzy hair and inch-thick glasses. He used to come to our performances, and he was the only person who ever looked me in the eye and said, "I get the feeling you're not really *in* these shows, Cynthia."

I blinked. *If I'm not really in these shows*, I wondered, *then where am I?*

"So where are you?" he asked.

After that, I avoided Richard.

Thirteen years later, Richard rides up to the café on a battered bicycle that has seen better days. When he sees me in the café window, his face cracks into a blinding grin. I blink mulishly, clutching my macchiato.

"Cynthia!" he mouths at the glass. He grabs a satchel off the back of his bike, nearly knocking it over in the process, and trudges into the café, dumping his worn canvas bag on the table with a *whomp*.

I lean over and hug him awkwardly, hoping I'll be able to manufacture an excuse to slip away soon because, frankly, I don't want to read his book. "It's a self-help book," he says apologetically, still shining that headlights-on-high-beam smile at my face. "I channeled it."

"You *what?*"

"Well, I didn't really write it, let's put it that way. It just came to me and I wrote down the words. Is that channeling?"

"How should *I* know?" I snap, peeved that he would imagine me an expert on channeling. "Are you channeling some dusty dead guy?"

"No, no, no. Nothing like that," he says, pulling a sheaf of lined yellow paper covered with illegible scribbles from his (macchiato-spattered) canvas bag. "I'm channeling Joan of Arc."

I cover my face with my hands. "You're channeling Joan of Arc, and you need to tell me about it—*why?*"

"I need to make sure it reads well for a modern audience. She tends to say things like, 'Those are my orders from my Lord.'"

"That doesn't read well for a modern audience, Richard. Trust me."

His eyes widen and he gets a dazed look on his face as he presses both hands into the sheaf of paper. "But she's telling me to write this book."

"Ignore her."

"You can't just ignore Joan of Arc."

"Oh, yes you can," I say snappishly, reaching for my macchiato. I am picturing Richard's face when he asked me, thirteen years ago, *So where are you, Cynthia?* I should have punched him then and there. Should have laid him flat.

He is blinking at me with puppy-dog eyes.

"Fine," I mutter, folding my arms across my chest. "Tell me about your book."

Richard's book is about hearing voices, and while I tend to hear voices myself, that isn't something I tell people—except, well, you, but I'll probably end up editing that part out.

"Haven't you ever heard a voice inside your head, Cynthia?" Richard asks.

"NO." I take a truculent sip of coffee. "You can get locked up for that kind of thing."

"Well, I have," he says. "And it tells me what to write."

I squint at him, envisioning Richard in a padded cell, doped up on Haldol.

"Will you read it?" he asks.

I stare at the mangled pages Richard thrusts at me, and I hesitate, afraid that his New Age dementia will rub off on me and I'll start channeling Attila the Hun. But those plaintive yellow pages reach out to me, whispering my name, and I can't help myself. It is, after all, a story.

"Fine."

As I read Richard's book, I consume a whole package of Oreos. *This book is terrible*, I think. Will I tell him this? Do I want my friends to tell me I write like a hyena? *I do not.* I will say, politely and sweetly, "Richard, I'm sure there's an audience for this book somewhere in the hidden valleys of southern Appalachia." Then Richard will go away for another thirteen years and I can return to the safety of my own questionable stories.

"*Mom!*" The cry, freighted with catastrophe, comes from Eliza, who is probably suffering from a twinge in her toenail or a lump in her thumb. "My cheeks are killing me," Eliza said just last week, and I burst out laughing. If nothing else, her ailments are entertaining. She's creative in her hypochondria. I sigh and head for the door.

"My earlobes itch," says Eliza without preamble, looking up from her cross-legged position on the kitchen floor. I, incompetent mother that I am, cackle.

"I'm serious, Mom. Is it cancer?"

"Cancer of the earlobes? That's a new one, sweetheart. Try moisturizer."

Eliza, not a big talker, is satisfied with this explanation and reaches for the cat. That's when I have the realization.

Writing is our appointment with the gods. We sit in our chairs and we pry open our hearts and we pray to the gods to carry us away. Like hang gliders, we wait for a wind we can sail away on. Never sure if the wind will come today or tomorrow, we trust that it will come. Waiting is our religion. We practice it earnestly, and when the gods show up, we leap into the air, soaring hundreds of feet above the ground, cruising the currents for all we're worth before crashing to the ground. Then we stand up, brush ourselves off, and wait, like obedient schoolchildren, for the next great gust to come along.

Richard's book isn't about Joan of Arc; it isn't even about hearing voices—it's about the art of flying. It's about waiting for something beautiful to come out of the sky and sweep you off your feet and carry you toward the sun. It's about writing that story the very best you can and polishing it like a river rock and showing it to people and feeling utterly grateful that it came to you. This book is Richard's river rock, and my job is to turn it over between my palms with all the reverence due to an act of creation.

I pick up the phone to call Richard. I need to tell him I love his book.

CHAPTER TWENTY

Acne, Heart Attacks, Rosacea

DAVID AND I GO AWAY FOR THE WEEKEND WITHOUT THE kids. It's been ten years since David and I have left the house without kids. With no one in the back seat, who are we? *What do we talk about?*

We drive in silence up the coast to Bodega Bay. "How do you think they're doing?" I ruminate, chewing my fingernail, when the real question is, *How are* we *doing?*

"Fine," says David, which is David's response to everything I could possibly think to ask him.

"What do you think of Bush getting elected?"

"Fine."

"What about those Cardinals yesterday, losing the Super Bowl?"

"Fine."

And my favorite, "What's for dinner?"

"Fine."

"Chopped or sautéed?"

It's come to that. He doesn't give my perseverations much thought, and that's okay. I just need him to pretend he's listening: the chin cupped in one hand, the slow blinking as if he's following my inscrutable logic. It's fine if he thinks about JaMarcus Russell. Or how much motor oil he needs for his next valve job.

I consider and reject several topics of conversation. *You don't need to talk,* I tell myself. *Talking isn't everything.* I picture those old couples at the restaurant who ran out of things to say to each other in 1956. The wife stares out the window, feigning fascination with the scenery, while the husband, like David, is perfectly comfortable not saying a word. It's a relief for him after listening to her jabber for forty years. *She finally ran dry,* he thinks. Talking is overrated, as far as men are concerned. They go to restaurants to eat.

"David?" I venture timidly.

The other useful word in conversations with your wife is—

"What?" he says.

"Maybe we need a hobby, or something we can *do* together. You know, like hobbyhorse racing or senior bowling."

"Fine," he says.

"What about yoga? Or Chilean fire dancing? Those would be fun. We could do ornithology."

"What's that?" Give him credit for variety.

"Never mind," I say, slumping in my seat. "It's just that I get so damn *uncomfortable* when we're not talking. I feel disconnected from you."

"Oh," he says, perking up. "I don't. Feel disconnected, that is." He lays a warm hand on top of mine. "Talking's overrated, honey."

Right.

Later that day, we go on a hike. I decide to try being quiet for a change to see if I can get comfortable with silence. Secretly, I know that David has something to teach me about this.

Help! I think after ten seconds. *I'm going to get bored! A fate worse than death!*

David doesn't *get* bored.

"Boredom is an exalted state," he likes to say, which means that if he did get bored, he would be exalted, but he doesn't, so how would he know? I feel an attack of the crabs coming on. Bored, disconnected, and grumpy, I trudge through the redwoods behind him.

Breathe, Cynthia. It's just silence.

Suddenly, I see Armani-Mom at the podium—the lights are dimming and the lecture is about to begin:

"Students and Faculty of Armani University," she exhorts. "There are several principles you'll need to know to navigate your way to a successful Armani life." She flattens a perfectly smooth strand of silver (not gray) hair and continues. "First and foremost, do whatever you need to do to get to a man's dick." She flashes a visual aid (which I will not describe) on the board behind her. "Second, have at least one orgasm a day. It's puritanical to have fewer. Besides, you'll get acne, heart attacks, and rosacea."

The students squirm but do not tear their rapt gazes from Armani-Mom's face. "And third, *never ever* let the conversation falter. Do not, for a moment, drop the conversational ball, or a bomb will detonate in the Society for Strategic Superficiality and everyone will die and evacuate all over your Aubusson carpet. It is *simply not done.* You must train yourself to always have something of interest to say. Consider as topics of conversation: the weather, the state of undress in current popular culture, the latest formulation of Campho-Phenique. Bring note cards if you must, or write on your arm. One woman I knew had the prime minister of Nigeria tattooed on her wrist, but unfortunately— she wasn't too bright—he had been overthrown by the time she dropped his name into the conversation."

The lights pop on, applause erupts, and I'm still left tramping along in utter, deafening silence behind David.

"What *is* a hobbyhorse, anyway?" I whinny.

"What?"

"I'm freaking out!"

"What the hell for? It's a beautiful day, we're on a hike, we're here together. Just relax, Cynthia."

Just relax. If I had a nickel for every time someone has told me to *just relax*, I'd own a hotel on the beach. I chuff with indignation, breaking out in a sweat and tripping over my own foot.

Okay. I get it.

I straighten my spine and drop my shoulders and take a deep breath, reminding myself that this is like meditation. You just have to pay attention. The playground monitor doesn't make a sound, but her smugness is thick as smoke.

Two hours later, we arrive back at the hotel without having said a word. "David?" I whisper like a kid after lights-out.

"What, honey?"

"I was pretty quiet, wasn't I?"

David turns around and shines the full light of his radiant smile on my face. He takes me in his arms, and I know, in that moment, that I am truly cherished. "You were great, honey. It was nice, wasn't it?"

Well. I wouldn't go that far.

"I've fired my muse," says my friend Deb the following Tuesday, "because she's a fake."

"You say that every year."

"It's true every year."

I sip my coffee substitute and ponder our relentless quest to find the true muse, not the one that exhorts us to Be Somebody but the one that insists that we keep our appointments with the gods. "Are you hiring a new one?" I ask.

"Not unless I'm a hundred percent sure she's the real deal."

"How will you know?"

"That's just it, I always think she's the real deal until she starts telling me what a genius I am. Then I have to get rid of her all over again. It's a constant upgrade."

"I keep having dreams that I'm trying to get somewhere," I tell her. "I have this freakish sense of urgency and I'm scrambling to get there in spite of sandstorms, collapsing bridges, and dead ends."

"Where are you trying to get to?"

"Just *there*. I don't know where *there* is. There are hundreds of family members milling around like cockroaches, getting in my way, and I can't get anywhere!"

"Sounds horrible," says Deb, and I can hear her running water in the sink. "How's your current book coming?"

I perk up like a hamster, my nose quivering wetly. "It's so weird, Deb. The book is about knowing that this—this moment—is enough, and yet everything I write is about how far I am from that. I'm always struggling to be somewhere else. It's like I know what the story is supposed to be about, but what I'm writing is a complete contradiction."

Deb is silent. I think she may have finally realized that I am a lunatic and now she will hang up on me forever. I sit up, preparing to act normal and pretend I never said any of that. I will talk about the mortgage crisis, I decide; I will compare toothpaste flavors.

"I think," she says slowly, and I sink back into the sofa with a sigh of relief. When Deb gets this lugubrious tone in her voice, she's about to say something that will squirrel into my brain and change my life forever. I tuck my legs under me and wait.

"I think you have to keep trying to get there, Cynthia. Keep trying as hard as you possibly can until you realize you've been there all along. *That's* what your book is about."

I hear a gush of air from somewhere nearby, and it takes me a full minute to realize that it came out of me.

CHAPTER TWENTY-ONE

It's Enough

DESPITE ALL MY EFFORTS, I'M STILL A WALKING TORNADO of doubt and worry. There must be something I can do. I sign up for a weeklong retreat at a meditation center, and as I drive across the bridge to sunny Marin County, I think, *A week should do the trick.*

I drive to Spirit Rock Center and lug my enormous bag full of belongings (pills and ointments, socks and notebooks, hair products, face products, skin products, products to prevent every imaginable disease that might arise in the course of six days) up the hill and stow it all away in my monastic little room. Tingling with excitement, I race over to the meditation hall and plunk myself down on my cushion. *I'm ready.*

I wait.

And I wait.

I try to breathe, twitching on my hard little (did I mention uncomfortable?) cushion as I wait.

I try to ignore my mind, which is drumming its fingers on an imaginary tabletop, while I wait.

I try to overlook the fact that *everything* hurts while I wait. Parts of my body that I didn't even know were parts of my body hurt. Like the floor. That hurts. And my pants, they hurt. My teeth hurt. My cerebral cortex hurts so badly my eyeballs are hot. *It's okay*, I tell myself in a serene voice. *You will be blissed out tomorrow. It takes a while.*

The next day is worse. My joints are sore from the day before. My legs don't bend anymore. My back is locked into permanent spasm, and my brain has become a weapon of mass destruction. *When exactly*, I ask myself in a cloying voice, *do the peace and quiet kick in?*

NEVER, croaks my brain in jubilation. *You are chopped liver!*

The image is alarming and I suppress it quickly, producing an alternate fantasy of lunch, which will be organic and delicious. I squirm on my cushion, trying to ignore the red-hot throbbing in my butt bones.

Why do people do this?

I paste a serene smile on my face in case anyone is looking. They're supposed to have their eyes closed, but it's important to keep up appearances. One must look as if one has transcended all physical pain and mental scarification. A tiny condescending smile implies this best.

But as I wriggle on my cushion, trying to look enlightened, I think, *I never would have signed up for this if I'd known it would involve six days of unrelenting agony. I want to go home. I want a taco and a glass of beer. I want a hot bath and a bad TV show and something sugary and artery-clogging and pulsing with colors that don't appear in nature.*

I continue to sit there. And a funny thing happens. As I sit for hours, scrutinizing my own discomfort, taking inventory of every broom closet in the familiar household of my pain, I start to give up. I give up trying. I give up hoping. I give up the aspiration that my life will be miraculously realigned in six days. I give up on that juicy, runny feeling of calm I have paid good money for, and in that very moment, the pain evaporates.

When you stop struggling, the playground monitor whispers, *there is peace.* I remember the beach in Hawaii, I remember the mountain lion, I remember the vision quests that opened my heart because I was able to slow down.

Peace.

I'm sitting on my cushion, and the pain is gone. The discomfort has vanished, and I realize something: sitting here and listening to my mind run its catastrophic scenarios is only the first step.

If you can listen in without resisting what you hear, with kindness even, the door opens. You walk through that door and find yourself in a wide-open space. There may be a dark corner where all your dramas are still gibbering away, *but it's not scary because, in this wide-open space, you're willing to love all of it.* Every monster, every fear, every pain . . . you embrace them, and you see that they are harmless.

Pretty soon, you hear birds singing. The room becomes bright and sunlit. There you sit, watching the burlesque of your own consciousness with a smile on your face, and it's like watching a TV show. A noisy, cacophonous, wondrous TV show. The pain, the striving, the desire, the delight. A crazy, beautiful spectacle that contains all the contradictory expressions of life. You might realize that the singing birds and the gibbering dramas are the same. There is no difference at all.

When I go back to my dorm that night, I'm aware of a stereo

track in my head: there's noise and mental arguments, like a perennial lawyers convention, and behind it, there is silence. The silence is its own track, humming underneath everything else. The silence is where we are alive, where we are connected, where there is no fear. The silence is joy. For the first time in many years, I sleep deeply without thoughts.

When I drive away from Spirit Rock, I'm not enlightened, but I'm quiet inside. I don't believe in my own catastrophes. I go home with a shrug of my shoulders and tell David, "It wasn't a big deal." Then I make myself a cup of tea, noticing every movement of my fingers as they prize the teabag from its wrapper, sensing the salivation that occurs just before I raise the warm cup to my lips, inhaling the sweet aroma of berries. I pause before I drink, and I feel grateful.

And you know what? It's enough.

"I don't need regular sessions," May says over the phone. "I just need to come in once or twice to get some tools. I've been a mess lately."

"That sounds hard," I sympathize. "How about next Tuesday at four?"

"I'll be there."

I hear so many stories. I hear about women who have given everything to their children and have nothing left for their husbands or, more critically, for themselves. "What do *you* want?" I ask these women. I hear couples that say unforgivable things to each other, breaking something far more fragile than their marriage vows. "How do we put the pieces back together?" they ask.

Every question is a mirror. I have to do the same work that they do; otherwise, I don't have the right to sit across from them.

"My husband is going to die," says May the following day. "And I don't know how to live on my own."

Do I know how to live on my own?

May has begun grieving even before Jim dies. We talk about grief, and how it unravels you, and I ask, "What do you love to do?"

She pauses, her brow knotted. "I don't know," she admits. "I haven't loved anything since my kids were little."

Why do we give up what we love?

"What brings you home to yourself?" I ask.

"I used to paint." She looks shy, almost embarrassed.

I invite her to visualize a big, empty canvas and a palette of paints. Carefully—the internalized voices of my Counseling Center supervisors muttering, *Don't do too much*—I ask her, "What does the canvas want you to do?"

She takes a breath. After a moment, she releases a huge rush of air, and I can see she's had a realization.

"It wants me to paint trees." She laughs. Her eyelids flicker over the images in her mind. "There will be times when I'll miss Jim so much I won't be able to paint, but I have to keep on living."

"You have to keep on living," I echo May's words.

When May leaves my office, I stay rooted in my chair. *What have I given up that I once loved?*

CHAPTER TWENTY-TWO

She May Be Crazy, She May Be Dangerous, but She Is Going to Dance

THE THEATER.

The thought dive-bombs my head like a mosquito. *I used to love the theater.*

It's okay to drop things, I tell myself. *It was okay to move on.* But, as Socrates would say, this is part of my unexamined life, and as I drag the covers over my head later that night, I know it's not the truth. I ran from the theater just as I ran from my mother's contempt and I ran from Stallion and Melissa. I run. It's what I do.

As if stricken with an exotic sub-Saharan rash, I squirm all night and into the next day. I squirm in my chair during my client sessions until Saturday rolls around and David and I drive across the bridge to see a student performance that Bob of the Hawkeyes has directed. There, sitting in the auditorium of Tamalpais High School watching teenagers perform Bob's original play, I stop twitching and stare, my mouth hanging open, at the stage.

Bob has been teaching theater at the high school, and the second half of the evening is the show he created with the kids. But first, I sit through the first half—scenes from Shakespeare—in which seventeen-year-olds bloviate, giving voice to the unfathomable depths of Shakespeare's language without a lick of life. They have no idea what they are saying.

"Nothing worse than fake British accents," I mutter as the audience claps dutifully.

After the intermission, nineteen bodies fly onto the stage. Tall bodies, thin bodies, round bodies, clumsy bodies, and balletic bodies catapult across the floor, their feet bare, their faces—for the first time that evening—*cracked open*. I hold my breath. Their words erupt from the bleeding heart of language, a place accessible even to seventeen-year-olds, because it is the language of the body. It is the language of raging hormones and pointless lust and stupid mistakes, the language of violence and error. I sit up in my chair, my heart jigging in my chest, aware that something shattering is taking place. I may be having a heart attack.

They claw at the stage with feral hands. They are possessed. They shoot through the air and collapse, dying of love, and a mortal battle ensues. The seventeen-year-olds are translucent, shining with sweat.

That's when I remember what it felt like to be possessed. To dance with the gods. Unfettered and ecstatic. Tears blur my vision as the kids hurtle across the stage. They are exponentially more powerful than they could ever be in the hallways of their school, in their mothers' kitchens. They are elemental forces of nature, and I am elemental along with them. When the house lights come up, I am out of my chair and I am yelling. I am yelling for their grace, and their brokenness, and their descent into the wildness we have all forgotten.

I am yelling for the theater.

The next day, I pick up the phone and call Joya.

Joya teaches theater, and she knew me back in the days when I was a performer. Okay, so maybe I was tossing myself at walls in a self-flagellatory frenzy, but I was also a good performer. I remember it like a long-ago dream.

"I quit the theater," I tell her, my throat squeezing out the words. "But I want to be able to move like I used to." There is a pause. I can hear her wondering what it is I really need, and I consider hanging up quickly in hopes that she will think this is a crank call.

But I go on. "I'm frozen," I explain to her. "Something happened to me then, and I'm afraid to move." I cough, trying to loosen the tightness in my vocal cords. "Can you help me?"

We meet at a dance studio in San Francisco where I performed long ago, an echo of the deep-buried past. I am as nervous as a pig in a bacon factory. I gulp and climb the dusty wooden stairs, and when I reach the top, Joya is waiting for me.

"I saw you perform many times," she tells me. "I never understood why you stopped." When I don't respond, she takes a breath. "Why don't you just move around," she suggests. "Warm up a little."

My body feels awkward, like a piece of furniture. I stretch my arms and legs, and my mind tells me that it's time to go home and stop making a fool of myself. *This can only end in ruin.* But my muscles start to remember. My muscles, no longer traitors, move with liquid ease, and I glide through the air as if my sails are unfurling. *I remember.*

Nothing stops me. Whatever stopped me all those years ago has dissolved, and nothing stops me now. I am dancing and shouting with all of my voice, and I am flying. I tell a story that is part dance and part confessional, and by the time I finish, Joya is standing up, clapping enthusiastically.

"Well!" she says. "You're clearly not frozen."

I look at her and I laugh because a door has opened. The door to the attic has been unlocked and Mrs. Rochester has been set loose. She may be crazy and she may be dangerous, but she is definitely going to dance.

We schedule another meeting. We are going to make theater.

"I realized what the matter was," I tell my friend Deb as I settle into the couch for our Tuesday-morning phone call.

"What?"

"I was doing theater for the wrong reasons."

"We do everything for the wrong reasons when we're twenty."

"Then we do a better job for the wrong reasons when we're thirty, and an excellent job when we're forty, and finally, when we're fifty, we realize we've become cardboard impersonations of ourselves."

"At least we have a few years left to change all that," Deb observes. I hear the sound of her refrigerator door opening. It's lunchtime in Vermont.

"I've been doing it for *them*," I tell her. "I don't want to do it for them anymore."

"It's especially hard not to do it for them in the theater because they're staring at you from the front row."

"Here's the thing," I tell her. "I'm going to invite an audience for the first time in ten years, and I'm going to perform, but I'm not going to do it for *them*. I'm going to do it for me. Does that make sense?"

"It's about time," says Deb, my muse and my friend through career changes and diapers, through failure and redemption. Then she says something I will never forget.

"It's time," she says, "for you to forget about the big impressive person you wish you were and do the small and precious thing that you love."

"I've been painting," says May, settling onto the couch. "It's not easy because I'm caring for Jim full-time now, but I made a studio out of our daughter's old room, and sometimes I just go in there and sit. I breathe in the colors."

"That's wonderful, May," I tell her. "What a gift to yourself."

"I know," she says. "When I can't sleep, I go in there and paint tiny canvases that only take me an hour or two. I've started a series. Do you want to know what I call it?"

"Absolutely." I smile. "What do you call it?"

"Resurrection."

CHAPTER TWENTY-THREE

It Was Never About Your Mother

I AM GOING TO HAVE TO LET THIS ONE GO.

This is the email from my agent. She is giving up on trying to sell my third book. I feel as though I've been hit by a train. I saw it coming, a black, roaring shape with one cyclopean headlight, and just as I entertain thoughts like *this will only hurt for a minute*—*whoooomph*, I am demolished. I've been rejected again, for the five thousandth time. I'm actually surprised by the pain —it's so sharp I can't swallow. I thought I was writing for the right reasons, without expectation, but this rejection catapults me into the old freefall of worthlessness. I'm still a nobody.

I decide to quit writing. I'll vacuum the bath mat and comb the cat and be Supermom for the kids' summer vacation. *How hard can that be?* I buy a brand-new sixteen-gallon spaghetti pot with industrial-sized handles, and, armed with recipes for *pasta alla puttanesca*, I whiz up to the cabin prepared to mother the hell out of my children and anyone else who happens to drive by. I make dinner for twenty-two members of the fire department and invite people I barely know over for lunch. I fling myself into non-writer mode like a kamikaze pilot, spewing flames all the way to the ground.

"I babysat for Jack today," Eliza informs me. She's ten years old, and this is her first paying job. "He had to put out twenty fires."

"Oh?' I ask, chopping spinach. "How did he manage that?"

"He peed on them. He didn't understand why I couldn't pee on the fires like he did." Eliza laughs and gets the hiccups, like she did when she was a baby. She used to hiccup so hard in utero that I felt her bouncing off my belly walls.

I wrap my arms around my daughter and sense her small body so alive with possibilities, and I think, *This is better than getting published. This is real.*

"Ow, Mom. You're squishing me." She pulls away. "I'm going to the store." And she's gone.

I stand there for a moment. *I've lost my way.* And then I remember an email from a friend who is taking a writing group to Tuscany in October. *Do it,* hisses the playground monitor. *Go to Italy.* I decide then and there. I'll take two weeks off from work and I'll go. I'll remember why I wanted to write in the first place. Italy will remind me of all the reasons I cared.

Staring out the kitchen window at the light slanting across the trunks of the Jeffrey pines, I imagine myself in a café with a leather-bound notebook and a good pen, and suddenly agents don't matter, publishers don't matter. All that matters is my good pen and the millions of brilliant ideas that swarm through my head demanding to be written down under the coarse Italian sun. *I've forgotten the point of it all,* I think desolately. *Italy will remind me what it was.*

On the plane, I feel excited. Despite carts jostling in the aisles, terrible movies no one would pay to see, crabby flight attendants, and even crabbier passengers scrunched up like pretzels in seats too small to accommodate a gnat, I am euphoric. *I'm going to Italy*, I chortle. *I'm going to find the answers I need.* Perhaps you have a sense of foreboding here, but I am too blind to notice.

Arezzo. Italian words trip from my tongue like parakeets in flight; narrow, leaning buildings, each older and more ruined than its neighbor; monster stones pitted with centuries of improbable survival. There are women in tight skirts and tippy high heels, too glamorous for the supermarket, and children running beloved in the streets. No culture adores its children as the Italians do—this love, from birth, defines the nation, a nation of lovers, a nation of beloveds. Lovers pressed together at every corner, on benches, on parapets, against church walls: kisses that never end. And bells! Irrational bells clanging insanely from morning till night, at seven minutes after the hour or fourteen minutes before the hour—never logical—bells that jangle your brain to insist that you wake up and remember something of great import. Even the bell ringer has forgotten what it was, but he hauls on the ropes like a drowning man, celebrating what he's forgotten with a great clashing din.

To love! he clangs.

"Laura is in the hospital," says Maria, the hotel manager. "She cannot teach the class."

I stare at Maria's lipsticked mouth. Our writing teacher is sick.

"Here is Kirby." Maria points to an elfin woman wearing incongruous red spectacles. "Only two of you now. What will you do?"

Will we turn around and head home? Will we wait to see if Laura pops out of bed? Or will we let Italy decide?

Kirby shoulders her ten-pound tote bag as if she's marching off to war. "We'll get a glass of wine," she announces, trampling indecision in her no-nonsense boots. I follow her to the *enoteca*. Kirby, it turns out, is a quick-witted Canadian lawyer who wears MC Hammer pants. Her eyes flash as she peppers the waiter, in textbook Italian, with questions about Arezzo. She pulls out a tiny Moleskine notebook to take precise, lawyerly notes on his recommendations. This woman is ferocious about her pleasure, and I find myself pulled, mesmerized, in her wake.

"I'm staying," I announce before I've even lifted my glass. We are sitting in a tiny wine bar off the big square in Arezzo. The shelves gleam with dusty bottles of Tuscan wine like a cozy, packed library. *Wine is like books*, I think. *Each bottle contains a story.* "I'm going to stay here and write for a week, whatever happens with Laura." I hoist my glass.

"I'm staying, too," she says. "I've already told Maria." She clinks her glass against mine. "Here's to our teacherless writing workshop." We drink to the adventure ahead, letting the deep, salty earthiness of Italian wine go straight to our rational North American heads.

The following morning, we sit at a café on the square as first light breaches the church steeple and yawning shopkeepers stagger out to unfurl their awnings.

"Let's write about something on the square," I suggest, and we open our notebooks. The sun hits my face and the café owner brings me a cappuccino, and I write about a young woman sprawled on the church steps across the square. She has nowhere to go and nothing on her agenda. For her, the sun, the pitted stone steps, the just-awakening square are enough. She lounges in her life, contented, while I race, huffing along an unseen trajectory. I watch her stretch and shed her jacket in the morning sun; she leans her elbows back against the steps and tilts her face into the light, and I imagine, for just a moment, how it would feel to relax like that. A pause, like a moth, flickers across my awareness.

Kirby, in true lawyerly fashion, writes about the eighteenth-century judicial courthouse across the square.

"I'm glad," I admit as we spoon foam into our mouths with tiny Italian teaspoons, "there's no teacher to tell us what to write."

"Well, never having written anything before, I'll have to surrender to your expertise," Kirby says. We leave a few coins on the table and head for a park. "Lead on."

In an enclosed rose garden, we write about opportunities we've passed up in our lives. We listen to each other's words and peel back the lies. When we get hungry, we stroll across town.

Every meal is a feast of fresh olive oil and garlic mixed with whatever vegetables, mushrooms, and pasta are available to the chef that day. The pleasures of Italy are making me fat and happy. They have taken hold of me and shaken out the cobwebs, loosened my worries and controls, and tossed me into a sea of indulgences that most sane Californians would fiercely abjure: strong coffee, thick wine, fatty pork, rich cheese, and even the occasional stolen inhalation of malty cigarette smoke in the air. These things would kill you outright in California, but in Italy, you glide in a bubble of immunity, protected by the shiny Roman gods of pleasure.

We take trains and buses to smaller towns, tramping through Cortona and Orvieto and Poppi in our sensible North American walking shoes (no teetering high heels for us). We write in vineyards and churches, perched on stone walls. The words flow effortlessly onto the page, pouring out of us in end-less delight like Tuscan rivers tumbling over hillsides. Each day unfolds in a feast of regeneration until Kirby announces, "This is all well and good, but I want to write a book."

With a thump, our happy days go dark. Laura rises from her sickbed to contribute enormous sheets of blue paper and an exercise that will germinate a book idea. I take the paper with shuddering fingers, knowing in my bones that whatever I am searching for in Italy, it's not another book. I've written six books. What I need to find is my purpose.

We go to the fifteenth-century library across the square and sit at a table in the sunny courtyard, unfurling the huge sheets of paper. The sun beats down on my back as I sit there, my pen hovering uselessly over the page, while Kirby scrawls a landscape of interconnected thoughts across hers. The playground monitor mutters in my ear: *This is not the answer.*

"Lunch," announces Kirby.

Kirby and I eat our pasta in silence. We've lost our open, wondering minds. We worry over our projects, feverish with effort. We still travel to outlying towns, walk their cobbled streets, and stroke the lean Italian cats, but we are blindly focused now. Separate.

Then, one night, I climb into my crisp sheets, expecting the rush of delight that late-night solitude brings, and I feel the sudden, clammy grip of despair. *There is no point*, I tell myself, *to any of this.*

I scuttle under the sheets and clamp my eyes shut. But the feeling won't go away. It tells me that I'm a fool for writing, that I've come to Italy to find my purpose but it isn't here. It isn't anywhere. I should just give up. *When you gave up the theater*, it reminds me, *you stopped hurting.*

It's true. I didn't have to keep trying. I didn't have to keep failing.

The following morning, as we near the end of our retreat, our teacher drags herself from her sickbed to check on our progress.

"I'm going to quit writing," I blurt. Kirby and Laura stare at me as if I've grown a third eyeball. I blush sharply, having had no intention of making this a public proclamation. "What's the point?" I sigh, and my eyes fill with tears. I am furious with myself.

Kirby and Laura scrutinize me as if I've been possessed by an alien, and I want to sink below the cushions of my chair. "It's just an existential crisis," I mutter. "Nothing to worry about." I want them to shake me, to yell at me, to make me change my mind. I want them to care. I slash tears from my chin. "I quit the theater twenty years ago," I tell them, blowing my nose. "It's what I do." I blink. "I run away from what I love."

The silence is thick, and no one has anything to say. It's not their place to tell me to keep writing, although I long for them to do that. This is my turning point, and I'm unable to turn. I don't know any other option besides escape. I want another option, but I can't see it. I am frozen in my chair, tears blurring my vision. But Laura and Kirby are helpless in the face of my hopelessness, and I'm sorry I brought it up. Poor Laura is fresh from her sickbed and Kirby is, for once, without words.

"It's all right," I say at last. "I'll figure it out."

We stand up, and for a moment, no one speaks. Then we head for the door. Laura will return to her bed, and Kirby and I will go our separate ways. All the while, the question keeps jangling in my head. *What's the point? What's the fucking point?*

I stumble into the little church at the back of the square; not the big, fancy one where Sunday mass collects crowds of people but the empty little church that has no frescoes and no stained glass, just a few plaster saints loitering around the periphery looking bored. I sit on the hard pew and stare straight ahead at the simple wooden altar. An old man is on his knees a few pews ahead of me.

What's the point, I ask the saints, *of all this trying?* I am feeling sorry for myself. Clutching a ratty Kleenex, I feel like an orphan, abandoned and forgotten.

Praying for an answer.

Nothing moves.

The bells from the big church across the square start clanging like the irate honking of New York City cab drivers.

I continue to wait as grief collects under my breastbone like a fist.

Then, bowing their cracking heads, the plaster saints begin to whisper.

"There is no point," says Saint Jerome.

"Never was a point," agrees Saint Francis.

"Never will be a point," murmurs Saint Donatus.

They stare down at me, raining dust from their fourteenth-century shoulders like dandruff.

I glare at them, my mouth thinning to an angry line (this is not what I want to hear), but their words worm their way into my brain. Closing my eyes, I try to figure out what's happening to me. An unfamiliar recognition is stretching up the length of my spine.

"Stop looking for a point," Saint Francis says.

That's when the playground monitor finally breaks through the static. *I've been trying to tell you this all along,* she murmurs.

And suddenly, I get it. I've been struggling my whole life to find an answer. I tried theater, I tried writing, and I even became a therapist in order to feel that I had purpose, that I had value. But they were all just ways to run from my own emptiness. Theater is fine, writing is fine, therapy is fine (and good), but they are not the answer. The answer is right here. Right now. Inside me.

I make a weird noise, and the old man jumps up and shuffles out the door. Sitting here alone, I contemplate all the ways in which I've clawed at the world for approval, the fruitless ways in which I've aspired to be seen, when all along, the approval was not external. *I told you,* whispers the playground monitor. *It was never about your mother.*

"Oh, shut up."

I sit quietly for a long time, listening to the pigeons gossiping in the eaves, and the silence is familiar, like an old friend. I notice that my heart has unclenched and I'm no longer folded in on myself. I notice that my breath has become deep and regular. I feel altered, and it occurs to me that this is what one hopes for in church. I cast suspicious glances at my (now silent) saints.

Then I pull my notebook from my bag and start to write. The truth that has been banging me on the head all my life sinks in and enters my blood. *Stop struggling. What you need is right here. Right now.* I've known it before, but this time is different. The words flow from my pen like water from a spring, and I sit in that church until afternoon shadows slant deep across the floor and I have filled more than twenty pages. I am unusually calm. My despair has vanished to the place where despair is born from— the dark belly of the hungry mind—and my mind isn't hungry for anything other than this moment. I am sufficient. There is no one to please and no one to tell me what to do. For the first time that I can remember, my inside self and my outside self are the same. I've found my voice. I am cruising the currents of the gods.

I stand up, brush off my skirt, and shoulder my bag. Sliding out of my pew, I notice the angle of light falling through a dusty window, and I smile. The light is beautiful here, rosy and ancient.

With a wink for my saints, who will hold their plaster tongues until the next supplicant arrives, I push open the fifty-pound fourteenth-century door and step into the olive-scented sunlit afternoon. My playground monitor (or is it me?) whispers, *What's for lunch?*

CHAPTER TWENTY-FOUR

A Trail of Crumbs

I FLY HOME FROM ITALY AND CLIMB INTO MY BED IN a jet lag coma, then wake to hear David making breakfast for the kids. I've already told you this part. Eliza's best friend, Celeste, has slept over, and the girls are catapulting their scrawny ten-year-old bodies over the furniture like psychotic hamsters. When the thudding soundtrack of their acrobatics has fully roused me, I sidle into the kitchen to grab a cup of coffee substitute.

That's when I see David at the stove flipping pancakes, and I understand that for David, every act is an act of love. I stand there, unable to move, and realize that David's rooms are empty, just like Adyashanti's. If he's flipping flapjacks, chances are he's not doing anything else at the same time, whereas I would be calculating the life expectancy of a gnat, or the mean distance between Bombay and Hiroshima, or the likelihood of my ever getting famous. For David, the flipping of the pancakes is enough. When your attention is that uncluttered, it's love.

I allow David to make me a mess of pancakes, and I eat every single one because I suddenly understand: it's all about love. Pancakes are about love, getting up early to feed the children is about love, pouring maple syrup you've specially warmed in the microwave is about love. Just standing there and smiling at a woman with the hair of an insane person and the fetid breath of Sunday morning is pure love.

The sunlight slicing through a rainy morning is definitely about love, and the syrup-sticky faces of ten-year-old girls—love. Even my son downstairs, sleeping off an adolescence that would have devastated a lesser mortal, is a bright and softly breathing expression of love.

See? the playground monitor whispers.

"Oh." I plant a kiss on my daughter's rumpled head. Then I pull a ski hat over my untamable hair and we scramble to catch up with David and Celeste, who have plunged into the jungle behind Lawrence Hall of Science.

We climb hills and slide down dales, accumulating clumps of mud. We lose our balance and topple into each other in a slippery pile of Gore-Tex, then we clamber to our feet and climb another treacherous slope, giggling all the while.

"Shall we have sticks or leaves for dinner?" I call out to my tribe of muddy REI primitives from the southern slope of Lawrence Hall of Science.

"Sticks *and* leaves," replies David, the only one who never falls over. That's because he's an empty room and doesn't have mental furniture to trip over, like I do. Even Eliza and Celeste have tiny, child-sized furniture accumulating in their brains. We stub our toes and bark our shins against every edge.

"Or better yet," David amends, leading the expedition into the present moment, every step a new aliveness. "Let's add rocks and call it a feast."

And that is the moment—you remember this, perhaps—that is the moment when I know.

This is it.

I try to hold on to it. I scribble memos to myself. I stack my bookshelves with Buddhist, Sufi, and Native American treatises. I try to avoid falling back into my reactive, amnesiac state. It's not about remembering the answer I have found. It's about remembering the question. The question is not *how do I get recognized?* The question is *how do I live?*

I pick my kids up from school, and I wrap them in suffocating bear hugs before I allow them to get in the car. "What's up, Mom?" they ask, eyeing each other. They are evaluating my sanity.

"I love you." I start the car. "I just thought I should say it."

"We know, Mom." What they don't know is that I'm not saying it for their mental health. I'm saying it for my own. I'm saying it because it's time to say what is so. I am planting myself at the very center of this moment because it's all I have.

I'm a good mother. Eccentric perhaps, and a little insecure at times, but I have loved well. I have learned to love well—first my husband, then my children, and now, myself.

Joy, like a warm sun, radiates through my being as I drive home, where I will make snacks for my kids just like I did when they were four years old, and I'll watch them disappear into their rooms to commune with their devices. Then I will sit in my kitchen and listen to the birds.

So, yes, I've returned from Italy, and what I thought mattered doesn't matter at all. I no longer need to meditate furiously or go on a diet or win an award. I want to drink Italian wine and take vacations. I want to be with my family and see my clients and write a dozen more books. I want to gobble it all down like a feast I've been missing.

Even now, as I go downstairs to my computer, it's different. I don't need to be famous; I don't need to be Somebody. I have stopped chasing ghosts, but still I go downstairs. *Why?*

Because this is what I do. I work on my book. I send letters to agents. I revise my old manuscripts and rearrange words on a page because it's—quite simply—what I love.

Like a trail of crumbs, I've left signs for myself all along the way.

Like a trail of crumbs, my path leads only in one direction. Straight ahead.

Richard was right—you can't ignore Joan of Arc. You have to listen to the voice of your heart. Even if you end up like burnt toast.

So here's what I can't ignore:

Writing saved my life as a child and brought me back to life as an adult. It is my life. And so is my family, and my cabin, and the mountains, and my husband with his clear brown eyes and my children with their not-yet-realized dreams and my clients with their cranked-open hearts. And so is *pasta alla carbonara* if it's done just right, and so are my friends, and my cats, even if they do shed glommy fur all over the duvet (the cats, not the friends). And so is the theater. Your life is what you love. So do it. Do it anyway. Don't run away.

I'm lying in bed staring at David, who is fast asleep, his lips parted, his eyes blinking in a dream. "You are so annoying," I whisper. "You really drive me crazy, you know that?"

David doesn't move.

"You just lie there without a clue as to what's going on," I tell him. "I've got whole universes of trouble getting ready to go to war inside me and you can sleep?"

He rolls over, licking his lips.

"You can just snooze away while a nuclear holocaust is getting ready to detonate in my brain? What about the children? What about the cat?"

David snores slightly, and I wrinkle my brow in disgust. "That just burns me up," I say. "What kind of a husband are you, anyway? Do you even *care* that I'm going to get cancer and end up like my mom, eating chocolate cake all day and watching soaps?"

David cracks a sleep-filled eye. "Turn those headlights down," he says. "Your brights are on." He takes a deep breath and risks a glance in my direction. "Hi, honey," he says. "How's your morning going?"

"Great," I say, and give him a kiss.

He smiles and emits a noise that's somewhere between a belch and a sigh. "Good," he says. He enfolds me in his warm, hairy, man-smelly arms and all my pulsing red crisis buttons flash off. A buttery spread of calm invades my chest and spreads to my outer regions, filling each of my fingers with warmth. "What's for breakfast?" I ask.

"I don't know," he says. "How about pancakes?"

Nothing Is Missing

I WANT TO END THIS STORY PERMANENTLY ROOTED in the knowledge that this is enough: this moment, this life, this experience. But I can't. It will come and it will go, and I will remember it and forget it every day of my life. I've been telling myself that I have to be enlightened to write the ending. I must be fully awake, or my story won't be instructive. It won't be the real deal.

But here's the thing: this—right now—is the real deal. It may be a sunny Wednesday afternoon in Berkeley. It may be a raging storm on a Scottish brae or a fishing pond in China. The real deal is right now. Wherever you are, hefting the weight of this book (or this device) in your hand and pushing your glasses up your nose (or not), this moment is your real deal, and it may not be enough, but it's all you have. So love it. Take care of it.

Maybe you wonder, too, late at night, when the calling owl has woken you up and you're squirming in the restless nest of your hot bed, what's missing from your life. Nothing. Nothing is missing. There's just a part of the human brain that dwells on missing things, like a Bureau of Missing Persons full of mustachioed agents running around with magnifying glasses and worrying about what they can't find. It's human. It's lovely and sad and messed up all at the same time.

Nothing is missing.

I'm going to end here. I'm going to save this document, step away from my desk, and go outside because the sun is bright and the air smells like peaches and I love the smell of peaches.

Thank you for taking this ride with me.

It may not be finished, but you know what?

It's enough.

ACKNOWLEDGMENTS

Heartfelt thanks to my beloved husband of forty-two years, David, and to Kyle and Eliza, who have been the world's best kids and have put up with my taking them public this year. Thanks to Jessie and Arthur for being family. Thanks to my initial readers and supporters in this decade-long endeavor: Deborah Gwinn, Mimi Seton, Patti Boucher, Joya Cory, Summer Brenner, Jill Moore, Judith Tripp, Laura Deutsch, and Lisa Dale Norton. Thanks to the team: Tommy Nolan, Signe Jorgenson, Lauren Wise, Brooke Warner. Many others read chapters and excerpts, and I am deeply grateful to each and every one of you for your support. Many thanks to the friends, family, and wildly creative theater colleagues I have mentioned here, and please remember that my recollections are utterly personal and subjective and not necessarily identical to the memories that live on in the minds of others.

Thanks to my many clients who were in so many ways my teachers. No clients have been reproduced in these pages, but aspects of some clients have been grafted onto aspects of others to preserve anonymity. Each one of you has been precious to me. All client names and conversations are invented. In addition, some characters have been compiled from several other characters and their names have been changed to protect the innocent.

.

ABOUT THE AUTHOR

Credit: Eliza Montana Photography

CYNTHIA MOORE is an award-winning playwright and performer who wrote and directed theater for over twenty years. A founding member of Otrabanda Company, she also worked in the Honolulu Theatre for Youth and the women's collective Lilith before joining the Blake Street Hawkeyes. In 1990, she left the theater to earn a master's degree in clinical psychology. She has now worked as a mental health counselor for twenty-three years, with a particular focus on the healing connection between spirituality and trauma. She has also taught numerous workshops in creativity, writing from the heart, and more. Cynthia lives in Berkeley, California, with her husband, David.

Looking for your next great read?

We can help!

Visit www.shewritespress.com/next-read
or scan the QR code below for a list
of our recommended titles.

She Writes Press is an award-winning
independent publishing company founded to
serve women writers everywhere.